You Strike A Woman, You Strike A Rock
Wathint' Abafazi, Wathint' Imbokotho

Written by Phyllis Klotz in collaboration
with Thobeka Maqhutyana,
Nomvula Qosha and Poppy Tsira

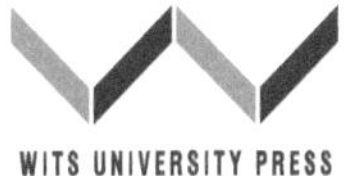

Published in South Africa by:
Wits University Press
1 Jan Smuts Avenue
Johannesburg 2001

www.witspress.co.za

First published 2021

http://dx.doi.org.10.18772/32021077205

978-1-77614-720-5 (Paperback)
978-1-77614-721-2 (Web PDF)
978-1-77614-722-9 (EPUB)

Project manager: Pat Tucker
Copyeditor: Pat Tucker
Proofreaders: Koliswa Moropa and Lisa Compton
Cover design: Hybrid Creative
Typeset in 10 point Minion Pro

To Lilian Ngoyi, Dora Tamana and Annie Silinga,
founder members of the Federation
of South African Women

Contents

Introduction by Sarah Roberts vii

Historical background xix

Glossary and translations xxvii

Images from the production xxxiii

You Strike a Woman, You Strike a Rock/
Wathint' Abafazi, Wathint' Imbokotho: The script 1

Prologue 3

Scene 1: The Marketplace 5

Scene 2: The Post Office 15

Scene 3: The Bus 21

Scene 4: The Dompas 28

Scene 5: The Train 30

Scene 6: The Workplace 33

Scene 7: The Farm 37

Scene 8: The System 41

Scene 9: The Hostel 46

Scene 10: The Father 50

Scene 11: The Foreboding Bird 56
Scene 12: The Blockade 60
Scene 13: The Student Protest 63

Discussion points 67

Introduction

WOMEN PROTEST IN LIFE AND ON STAGE

Sarah Roberts

When we watch, read, or play out scenes from *You Strike a Woman, You Strike a Rock* we become aware of how events from the distant past intersect with experiences of everyday living in more recent times. We also see a blend of historical incident with creative fabrication in a powerful theatrical expression of women's experiences within racist and patriarchal power systems. More than two decades after its first performances, the play – with its dedication to iconic historical female figures – has become part of a socio-cultural record as a rich testament to a specific period that commemorates the lives of hundreds of township women.

In Langa township outside Cape Town, a protest against the enforced use of the 'dompas' (passbook), a symbol of apartheid oppression and subjugation, took place on 4 January 1953. Dora Tamana, an anti-apartheid activist and trade unionist, spoke these words of defiance:

> We women will never carry these passes . . . We have seen unemployment, lack of accommodation and families broken because of passes. We have seen it with our men. Who will look after our children when we go to jail for a small technical offence [of] not having a pass?[1]

Three years later, on Thursday 9 August 1956, an estimated 20 000 women from all walks of life converged on the Union Buildings in Pretoria – the symbolic seat of the apartheid government – to hand over to Prime Minister J G Strijdom 14 000 signed petitions. These petitions spelt out the violations, indignities and constraints embedded in the pass laws and the impact the proposed amendment to existing legislation would have on the lives of black women and girls.

The Women's March was a powerful, affective and theatrical public intervention. As in theatre, some individuals featured prominently, while others remained anonymous. The march was led by Lilian Ngoyi, Helen Joseph, Albertina Sisulu and Sophia Williams de Bruyn, who are memorialised in statues erected in the Lilian Ngoyi Square, Pretoria. In 1956 the mass of 20 000 women stood in silence for half an hour, then sang 'Nkosi sikelel' iAfrika', followed by the women's struggle anthem, 'Wathint' abafazi, wathint' imbokotho, uza kufa!'

Public intellectual, academic and writer Njabulo Ndebele, in an essay entitled 'Actors and Interpreters',[2] probes the differences between efforts of ordinary people as agents of socio-economic and political transformation and those of radical theatre makers and artists. For him, ordinary people – activists among them, not just politicians – are 'the makers of history [who] bring about the actual material transformation of society'.[3]

He would describe every participant in the Women's March as an 'actor' because each of them, mobilised by a profound sense of responsible citizenship, engaged in civil protest. The sheer number of participants supports Ndebele's claim that the actors in the world of everyday life outnumber those he calls the interpreters. Interpreters, he writes, are commentators, theorists and artists, who either produce critical analyses and concepts to explain reality or create artistic texts that become part of a nation's cultural fabric. He makes the point, however, that 'artists, writers and musicians should never have an unrealistic view of the ultimate social significance of their work. Fiction can never replace politics in the total scheme of things.'[4]

Ndebele's ideas offer a way of understanding *You Strike a Woman, You Strike a Rock* with its display of the harsh realities of 1980s township life. The rallying cry of the women's anthem is embedded in this play devised by four women to express their insights and perspectives as 'interpreters' of those realities.

COLLABORATIVE AUTHORSHIP AND THEATRE MAKING

Phyllis Klotz, spurred by her commitment to theatre for development, formed the Young People's Theatre Education Trust in 1985. Thobeka Maqhutyana and Poppy Tsira were members of the Community Arts Project (1984–1985). Nomvula Qosha, a mother of four children, worked as a domestic servant and in a doctor's dispensary before she joined the creative team. Their lives provided much of the raw material for the play as a living testimony to the resilience of women in their roles as wives, neighbours, sisters, friends and mothers.

In devising the text, the collective drew on two forms of research. Scholarly accounts and perspectives (specifically those of sociologist and gender historian Cherryl Walker) were animated by the personal stories of township residents.[5]

This material was supplemented by visits to marketplaces to observe vendors and customers, which triggered improvisation exercises to shape characters, situations and action.

The women worked under difficult conditions, without financial support and amid mounting political unrest. Daily rehearsals took place from 9am to 4pm in the women's toilet at St Francis Cultural Centre in Langa until Klotz was no longer able to go to the township. The group was forced to relocate to the Community Arts Centre in Woodstock, Cape Town.

Their goal was to present the play at the National Arts Festival in Grahamstown, Eastern Cape, in July 1986. In early June, violence erupted in Crossroads and spread to the neighbouring areas of KTC and Nyanga, with faction fighting between the group known as the Witdoeke[6] and supporters of the banned African National Congress, Pan Africanist Congress and Azanian People's Organisation. Rehearsals stopped when Nomvula, who lived in KTC where violence was intense, could not be contacted for two weeks. Nonetheless, a work-in-progress was showcased at the Arena Theatre on the University of Cape Town campus. The production opened at the Grahamstown Festival, from which subsequent seasons and tours were launched.

The play maps the lives of three female characters, all informal traders selling their wares (chickens, oranges and vetkoek) at the side of the road. The experiences of these feisty breadwinners are interwoven with a vibrant tapestry of contemporary township life and a desperate struggle for material survival in which money is hard earned and every cent counts.

The gritty determination to overcome adversity is offset by the readiness to love and to embrace opportunities for enjoyment. Small achievements are joyously celebrated. Bantering rivalry for customers is interwoven with evidence of the impact of the pass laws as the women share details about their fractured family lives against the constant backdrop of a heavy police presence and student protest.

Routine trading activities are threaded through with flashbacks that trace Mampompo's journey from her Transkei home to join her husband, Nozulu, in Cape Town. The strategy of re-enacting vignettes from her past is complemented by storytelling: Sdudla, the oldest, and a struggle stalwart, describes (rather than relives) her memories of the march to Pretoria and shares her story with her fellow vendors and, notably, the audience.

She sets out to inculcate a political consciousness in those around her and challenges all those listening with a single line: 'The road to freedom is a long one, with many hills to climb.' The metaphor informs the structure and theme of the play, which is a kaleidoscope of the 'hills' to be navigated daily as a matter of survival.

The play shows that collective action and solidarity are a source of support, inspiration and endurance in confronting the violations and violence of 'ordinary' township life under apartheid. The audience is alerted to the enormity of personal sacrifice and the limits of suffering which temper the spirit of defiance. The representation of distinctly individual women, their personalities and perspectives, ensures an interplay of diverse identities and shows how public and private aspects of people's lives are intertwined.

As spectators, we witness the women's strategies for dealing with drunken Friday customers and their response to the demand to produce a trading licence. We hear of shared experiences in the workplace: dismissive abuse endured in menial domestic and corporate labour is voiced chorally. Jocular humour and courage texture the revelations of small details of everyday life: substituting 'Smarties' for explicit sexual references, Mampompo describes the ignominy of a reunion with her husband on the upper section of a bunk bed in the dormitory of a men's hostel. Her humiliation and outrage is revealed when the man on the bed below assumes that he too can claim her sexual services. This incident exposes the migrant labour system and the unnatural life of single-sex hostels and communal living.

SOUTH AFRICAN WORKSHOP THEATRE IN THE 1980S

The mid-1980s was a prolific period in South African theatre, which not only celebrated the craft of the individual playwright but promoted the work of the collective. Much of the theatre produced was unconventional and overtly opposed to the apartheid regime. Its origins were in the work produced in the 1970s by Athol Fugard, John Kani, Winston Ntshona and the Serpent Players (*Sizwe Banzi is Dead* 1972, *The Island* 1974) and by Gibson Kente (*How Long?* and *Too Late* 1974). Scripts, either written or printed, only followed months after the public performances.[7]

With the exception of the much-feted musical *Sarafina!* (1987) and *Born in the RSA* (1985), *Sophiatown* (1986) and *Township Boy* (1988),[8] many of the 1980s plays were created by – and focused on – black men and their experiences. They made for explosive, actor-centred theatre that featured all male casts, minimalist sets and costumes, multilingual dialogue and a heightened physicality in a performance style that integrated song, dance and mime.

The anti-naturalistic dramatic structure favoured stitching together sketches constructed around ubiquitous images of the 1980s – slogans, the toyi-toyi – and routine everyday activities. As in the relationship between traditional storyteller and listener (aware of the storyteller's capacity to transform and adopt multiple personalities), the acting method celebrated the performers' personalities and skills. Actors played multiple roles with full awareness of presenting a crafted performance to an audience whose presence they explicitly acknowledged as co-participants in the theatre encounter.

You Strike a Woman, You Strike a Rock incorporates these elements from an exclusively female perspective, counterpointing the dominance of male voices to expose the earlier apparent silence and invisibility of women. Albie Sachs had recorded a crucial point made at the seminal Arts and Culture Conference in Gaborone, Botswana, in 1982: liberation initiatives needed to address the 'triple oppression of black women of our country as members of an oppressed gender, oppressed nationalities and exploited class'.[9] Five years later, in Amsterdam, the Culture in Another South Africa Conference (14–19 December 1987) showcased this play – made by women and about women – to assert the place of women's theatre in the liberation struggle.

FEMALE VOICES IN HISTORY AND ON STAGE

Undercounted and unrecorded, women have left far fewer traces than men in the historical record. This is one of the most significant consequences of the negative

> cultural attitudes about women . . . [whose] lives became 'ahistorical', lived outside the world of masculine achievements.[10]

The term 'history' is presumed to refer to a systematic record of events and the people caught up in those events, preserved in writing as a public archive. The 'facticity' or integrity of information continues to be contested. As feminist and post-colonial criticism has increasingly shown, the discipline is fraught with questions of bias and perspective. The work of exposing patriarchal and Eurocentric biases in the historical record is ongoing. Subjective testimonies as narratives or as cultural artefacts – like this play – may well offer more reliable evidence of past events than conventional histories. Public stages – in theatres or elsewhere – give those who occupy them visibility and an audience, enabling them to become the 'makers of history'. *You Strike a Woman, You Strike a Rock* demands that we reassess the interplay of domestic and public worlds to reconsider what we acknowledge and value as 'achievements'.

The bristling energy of resistance captured in this play is a reminder that the rights safeguarded by the Constitution have been hard fought for by many anonymous ordinary citizens and unrecognised struggle icons who have passed on. Their fight should not be in vain.

Although women in the post-apartheid era appear to be less marginalised, theoretically protected by the universal rights entrenched in the Bill of Rights incorporated in the South African Constitution, they continue to grapple with the legacy of inequality and lack of material security.

Discrimination persists. Gender-based violence takes multiple forms, from domestic and sexual abuse to harassment in the workplace. Women still juggle domestic responsibility and employment.

The animated storytelling through intertwined acting, singing and dancing that is so central to the form and style of the play shows us the tools of survival and expression. The courage, determination and spirit of the characters Mampompo, Mambhele and Sdudla triumph: their voices soar in song while their energetic, dancing bodies celebrate the rhythm of life, defying the adversity symbolised by the 'plague bird' . . . 'hateful bird' . . . 'ugly bird' that circles overhead.

Song and dance bind individuals to each other and rhythm intensifies, emboldens and etches experience into memory in an encounter with living history. Like the monuments and statues that have been erected to honour the women of the struggle, the play commemorates the period in which it was made. Women's work in the form of routine activities along with determined commitment to fight for a better life is made visible. The play ends with the anthem as a declaration of defiance, resilience and hope.

This script is a blueprint that allows us to imagine robust interaction, flashes of lively humour and the will to overcome. The play sharpens both our sense of the present, with its continuing struggle for equality, and that of what our future might be.

Notes

1. 'Women's Resistance in the 1960s: Sharpeville and its Aftermath', South African History Online, accessed 22 February 2021, https://www.sahistory.org.za/article/womens-resistance-1960s-sharpeville-and-its-aftermath. For further reading on women in South African history, see Nomboniso Gasa, ed., *Women in South African History* (Cape Town: HSRC Press, 2007).
2. Njabulo S Ndebele, 'Actors and Interpreters: Popular Culture and Progressive Formalism', in *Rediscovery of the Ordinary: Essays on South African Literature and Culture* (Scottsville: UKZN Press, 2006), 73–100.
3. Ndebele, 'Actors and Interpreters', 83.
4. Ndebele, 'Actors and Interpreters', 97.
5. Cherryl Walker, *Women and Resistance in South Africa* (New York: Monthly Review Press, 1991).
6. The 'Witdoeke' were state-aligned vigilante groups whose name derived from the white scarves they wore around their heads or arms. They were particularly active in the Cape in May and June 1986.
7. In contrast, the early output of Fatima Dike (*The Sacrifice of Kreli* 1976, *The First South African* 1977) stands out as written by a woman prior to rehearsal. Gcina Mhlope's *Have You Seen Zandile?* (1986) focuses on the rural and urban experiences of girls and women, but is literary in origin, written in its entirety ahead of rehearsals.
8. Mbongeni Ngema; Barney Simon and the Company; Malcolm Purkey and the Junction Avenue Theatre Company; John Ledwaba and Christo Leach with the Mamu Players.

9. See Albie Sachs, 'Memorandum of the Symposium/Festival of South African Arts – Gaborone, 5–9 July 1982', accessed 25 February 2021, https://www.sahistory.org.za/archive/memorandum-symposiumfestival-south-african-arts-gaborone-5-9-july-1982.
10. Bonnie S Anderson and Judith P Zinsser, *A History of Their Own* (London: Penguin, 1988), xviii.

References

Anderson, Bonnie S and Judith P Zinsser. *A History of Their Own*. London: Penguin, 1988.

Gasa, Nomboniso, ed. *Women in South African History*. Cape Town: HSRC Press, 2007.

Ndebele, Njabulo S. 'Actors and Interpreters: Popular Culture and Progressive Formalism'. In *Rediscovery of the Ordinary: Essays on South African Literature and Culture*, 73–100. Scottsville: UKZN Press, 2006.

Sachs, Albie. 'Memorandum of the Symposium/Festival of South African Arts – Gaborone, 5–9 July 1982'. Accessed 25 February 2021. https://www.sahistory.org.za/archive/memorandum-symposiumfestival-south-african-arts-gaborone-5-9-july-1982.

South African History Online. 'Women's Resistance in the 1960s: Sharpeville and its Aftermath'. Accessed 22 February 2021. https://www.sahistory.org.za/article/womens-resistance-1960s-sharpeville-and-its-aftermath.

Walker, Cherryl. *Women and Resistance in South Africa*. New York: Monthly Review Press, 1991.

Historical Background

A PATRIARCHAL SOCIETY

Before 1996

The position of women, both black and white, in South Africa at the beginning of the 20th century was subordinate to that of men, who took all major decisions both in society at large and within the home.

African women did not enjoy the same legal status as men, under either the statuary laws or the enforced version of customary law. A black woman was deemed to be a perpetual minor in law and had no independent powers. Under customary law women remain perpetual minors under the guardianship of their father before marriage and their husband after marriage. A woman could not marry without the consent of her guardian. She had no contractual capacity and could not acquire or dispose of property. Black women in South Africa suffered from both the disability of apartheid and the oppression of gender and class.

After 1996

The Bill of Rights, a cornerstone of democracy in South Africa, recognises women as equal citizens enjoying all the rights guaranteed by Section 9 of the South African Constitution of 1996.[1]

Section 9(3) states:

> The State may not unfairly discriminate directly or indirectly against anyone on one or more grounds, including, race, gender, sex, pregnancy, marital status, ethnic or social origin, age, colour, sexual orientation, disability, religion, conscience, belief, culture, language and birth.[2]

Despite the progress made with regard to the rights of women and their access to education, they are still more likely than men to be employed in low-skilled occupations. This difference is driven by the fact that many are still employed as domestic workers, who experience the highest poverty rates and rely on income grants from government to make ends meet. Gender-based violence remains a profound and widespread problem in South Africa, having an impact on almost every aspect of life. It is systemic and deeply entrenched in institutions, cultures and traditions.

BANTUSTANS/'HOMELANDS'

The Transkei was one of the Bantustans[3] or 'homelands' established by the apartheid government, to which many black people were moved to prevent them from living in the urban areas of South Africa. The idea was to separate black people from white and give them the responsibility of running their own independent governments with limited powers, thus denying them protection and any remaining rights in South Africa.

Each of the ten 'independent homelands' was designated for a specific cultural group – for instance, the Transkei and

Ciskei were 'homelands' for the Xhosa people – but the lack of development in many of them left them almost entirely reliant on 'white' South Africa for their existence.

Farming was not viable because of the poor quality of agricultural land, soil erosion and over grazing. As a result, millions of black people had to leave the Bantustans to work, turning them into labour reservoirs.

THE PASS LAWS

Pass laws[4] have a long history in South Africa, dating back to 1760 in the Cape, when slaves moving between urban and rural areas were required to carry passes authorising their travel. Once the National Party government came to power in 1948, legislation was passed restricting the movement of black people.

The Native Laws Amendment Act of 1952 repealed the many regional pass laws and instituted one nationwide law requiring all black men over the age of 16 to carry passes when in white areas and stating that no black person could stay in an urban area for more than 72 hours without the correct documentation unless granted permission.

The pass or reference book (known contemptuously by those who had to carry it as the 'dompas') was similar to an identity document containing personal details, among them how long the bearer had been employed and sometimes the opinion of the employer (always a white person) of the conduct of the bearer.

The pass was, perhaps, the most hated of all the apartheid restrictions, having an impact, as it did, on every aspect of an individual's life. Desperation frequently drove people to breach the restrictions imposed by the pass laws in order to seek employment and support their families.

Section 10 of the Act set out the conditions under which black men were permitted to remain in urban areas. In terms of Section 10.1.A, if you were born in an urban area, for example, Langa, in Cape Town, you were permitted to live there and work in Cape Town without a permit. If you wished to visit someone in Stellenbosch, 40km away, you had to have a 72-hour permit. If, for instance, you were born in Cape Town but had a job in Stellenbosch, you needed a special permit in order to work there. In Stellenbosch you were classified as Section 10.1.B.

If you were not born in an urban area but in one of the 'homelands', or a rural area, in terms of Section 10.1.C you were not permitted to enter any urban area unless you had a legal contract to work there. If you left the area you were required to produce your dompas if approached by a police officer, and if you did not have the required 72-hour permit you were arrested immediately. The next morning you would appear in court and, if found guilty, you would be fined. You probably would not have the money to pay the fine and this would result in a prison sentence.

On average, a black person who was not carrying a dompas with the required permit would be sentenced to three months' imprisonment. During that period some prisoners were 'sold' to farmers, who exploited them. Once the sentence was served they were deported to their homelands.

POQO

In 1961 the Pan Africanist Congress formed a military wing they called Poqo[5] (meaning 'pure' or 'alone'), with the aim of overthrowing the white government. Unlike the African

National Congress's armed wing, uMkhonto we Sizwe, Poqo made no effort to avoid loss of life. The organisation drew most of its following from the Western Cape and Transkei.

THE WOMEN'S MARCH OF 1956

When the apartheid regime announced its intention to extend the pass laws to black women, organisations such as the Federation of South African Women began to mobilise women throughout South Africa to protest. On 9 August 1956, 20 000 women of all races, led by Sophia Williams de Bruyn, Helen Joseph, Lilian Ngoyi, Albertina Sisulu and Rahima Moosa, marched to the Union Buildings in Pretoria, where they intended to present a petition to then Prime Minister J G Strijdom. Strijdom did not appear and the petition was accepted by his secretary.[6]

THE PETITION

> We, the women of South Africa, have come here today . . . We African women know too well the effect of this law, upon our homes, our children. We who are not African women know how our sisters suffer . . . For to us, an insult to African women is an insult to all women . . .
>
> - That homes will be broken up when woman are arrested under pass laws . . .
> - That women and young girls will be exposed to humiliation and degradation at the hands of pass-searching policemen.
> - That women will lose their right to move freely from one place to another.

> . . . We, voters and voteless, call upon the government not to issue passes to African women. We shall not rest until we have won for our children their fundamental rights of freedom, justice and security.[7]

REPEAL OF THE PASS LAWS, 1986

Efforts to control the movement of black people proved to be a dismal failure. On 23 July 1986 the government, under President PW Botha, did away with the requirement that they carry pass books, although the pass system itself was not immediately repealed. The Influx Control Act, which had enabled government to prevent blacks from rural areas and homelands going to cities and industrial areas, was abolished.

STATE OF EMERGENCY

In 1984 violent political conflict and socio-economic upheavals erupted in South Africa. In spite of the government's attempts to squash it, the violence continued into 1985. In June of that year the government declared a partial State of Emergency in 36 magisterial districts in the Eastern Cape and the Transvaal (now Gauteng).[8] It gave the police powers to detain, impose curfews and control the media. In June 1986 the State of Emergency was extended to the entire country and hundreds of activists were detained. President P W Botha could now rule by decree and extend the powers of the army and police. Police units raided labour, church and political organisations and prominent leaders were arrested. Townships were patrolled by the army, which travelled in Casspirs – mine-resistant ambush patrol vehicles.

FOREFATHERS

Hintsa ka Khawuta, also known as Great or King Hintsa, was the fourth king of the amaXhosa nation. Ngqika ka Mlawu was the son of a Xhosa chief; King Moshoeshoe, also known as Mshweshwe, was Chief of the Bamokoteli; Dingane ka Senzangakhona, commonly referred to as Dingane or Dingaan, was a Zulu chief who became king of the Zulu Kingdom.

Notes

1. Constitution of the Republic of South Africa, 1996. 'Section 9', accessed 23 February 2021, www.gov.za/documents/constitution/chapter-2-bill-rights#9.
2. 'Section Nine of the Constitution of South Africa', accessed 25 February 2021, https://en.wikipedia.org/wiki/SectionNineoftheConstitutionofSouthAfrica.
3. 'Bantustan', Encyclopedia Britannica, accessed 25 February 2021, https://www.britannica.com/topic/Bantustan.
4. 'Pass Laws in South Africa 1800–1994', last modified 27 August 2019, https://www.sahistory.org.za/article/pass-laws-south-africa-1800-1994.
5. 'Poqo', last modified 26 July 2017, https://www.sahistory.org.za/article/poqo.
6. 'History of Women's Struggle in South Africa', last modified 11 January 2021, https://www.sahistory.org.za/article/history-womens-struggle-south-africa.

7. 'History of Women's Struggle in South Africa', last modified 11 January 2021, https://www.sahistory.org.za/article/history-womens-struggle-south-africa.
8. 'State of Emergency – 1985', last modified 10 March 2020, https://www.sahistory.org.za/article/state-emergency-1985.

Glossary and Translations

ah, tog	oh, dear
bankie	bench
bantwana bam	my children
baphi	where are they?
bhuti yiza	brother come
Dis al tyd om huis toe gaan – kom, kom	It's time to go home – come, come
dompas	reference book/pass
Halala!	Hurrah! [An interjective used to congratulate]
hamba	go
hamba kahle	go well
hamba sidenge	go you fool
hayi, hayi	no, no
hayi, hayi, mntan'am intloko yam iyaqaqamba	no, no, my child, my head is aching
hayi mfazi	no, woman
hayi suka	oh no
hayi uyandinyela	you are shitting on me
hayi, voetsak	no, voetsek
He mfazi zala uzoxoxa	Hey woman, give birth and you will start to argue
he wethu	hey friend
heyi hamba	hey go
hlala phantsi	sit down
home boy	a term used to refer to others (a male in this case) from the same community/area as the other person

ibhasela	reward
iinkuku zimnandi	chickens are delicious
imali ayitshisi	money does not burn
Inkom' ingazala umntu	[literal translation]: a cow can give birth to a human being [a figurative expression meaning something that would never happen]
iyawa ngala mapolisa	it is these police officers [again]
iyhuu	whew
kakade	already
kaloku mfazi	at this moment woman
Le nkuku ibaleka nemali yabantwana bam	This chicken is running away with my children's money
makhulu	grandmother
Makhulu sukuphusha	Grandmother, do not push
makoti	bride/newly-wed woman
Makoti ncancisa umntwana	Newly-wed woman feed the baby
Mamqwambi mfazi	Mamqwambi (this is a clan name) woman
maselandini	you thieves
mello yello	[township slang for a police vehicle]
mfazi	woman
molo	good day
mzabalazo	the struggle
nansti: laa ntaka	here it is: that bird
ndakunyisa	I will make you shit
ndiyayivala	I am closing it
ndiyayivula	I am opening it
ndiza kuyibulala	I am going to kill it
ngubani okuthumelela imali	who sends you money
Nkosi yam	my Lord/my Master

nkqo, nkqo	knock, knock
Nongqongqo	[name of a prison]
Noni sisi	Noni sister
Nanga esiza nganeno la mapolisa	Here are the police coming closer
Ozayo Makabongwe	Let the One coming be praised
qabakazi ndini	you illiterate woman
rha mnqundu wakho	sies, your arse
sana lwam	my baby
sapha	give it to me
Sapha loo bhotile yomntwana	Give me that child's feeding bottle
Shiya hom, hom bhasophani	Leave him, he must be careful
singene enkululekweni	[until] we achieve freedom
sisi	sister
sontombi	sister girl
Tata sukutshaya, intloko yam iyaqaqamba	Father do not smoke, my head is aching
thula	keep quiet
Tlola, ngwana re bone blumas	Jump, child, so we see the panties
toto	[a general name used to refer to a male, expressing endearment]
toyi-toyi	[a dance step typically performed during protests and marches]
tyhini	[an exclamation of surprise, awe or delight]
Uhleka ntoni?	What are you laughing at?
umama walo mntwana	mother of this child
umfazi ka	wife of
umthwalo	burden
unepasi wena	you have a pass
Unguyise esinya	S/he is just like his/her father

uphi	where is s/he?
uphi na lo mntwana	where is this child?
uphi umolokazana wakho	where is your daughter-in-law?
useKapa	she is in Cape Town
Uthi uza kumxhutha?	You say you are going to pluck off his feathers?
Uya kudliwa yindlala mntan'am	You will starve my child
uyazi	you know
Uzusithethelele	Please forgive us
vetkoek	[traditional South African dish made of fried dough]
yintoni mntase?	what is it child of my home?
woza mntwana	come, child
yam imke namanzi	[figurative expression meaning] [money] gone down the drain
ye Mqwathi, imali yam	hey Mqwathi, my money
yha	yes
yiza bhuti	come brother
yiza nalo	bring it

CHANTS AND SONGS

Le ntaka, Ndizal' abantwana, Ndizal' amakhosi Iya kufik' ibatshabalalise	This plague bird, I gave birth to children, I gave birth to kings This plague bird comes and destroys them
Iyhoho sotshona phin' amadoda? Halala!	Alas, where is our hideout men? Hurrah! [Halala is an interjective used to congratulate]
Sotshona phin' amadoda? Iyhoho sotshona phin' amadoda? Abantwana bethu sebelala ngendlala. Halala, sotshona phin' amadoda?	Where is our hideout, men? Where is our hideout, men? Our children go to bed hungry. Hurrah, where is our hideout, men?

Baphin' ooSilinga	Where are the Silingas?
Baphin' ooTamana	Where are the Tamanas?
Singene Enkululekweni	[Until] we have our freedom.
Lo Mzabalazo	This struggle
Sonyuka nawo	We are going forward with it
Singene Enkululekweni	[Until] we have our freedom
UMadlamini undimoshile	Madlamini annoys me
Ngokuthath' imali yabantwana bam.	For taking my children's money.
Ndiyamzonda, Ndiyamzonda	I dislike her, I dislike her
Ngokuthath' imali yabantwana bam.	For taking my children's money.
Unzima lo mthwalo	This burden is heavy
Woyis' amadoda	It has defeated men
Angeke soyiswe	It won't defeat us
Ke thina bafazi	Not us women
Hayi, Hayi	No, no
Nantsi imello yello	Here is a mello yello
Imello yello	A mello yello
Izosidubula	It is going to shoot us
Dubula	Shoot us
Balekani	Run away
Lenj' uBotha isiqhel' amasimba	This dog Botha undermines us like shit
Ngokubulalisa	As he causes us to be killed.
Isizwe sethu	Our nation
Sizozibulala ezi zinja	We will kill these dogs
Uzama ukwenzani xa Uthint' abafazi?	What are you trying to do when you strike a woman?
Wathint' abafazi, wathint' imbokotho	You strike a woman, you strike a rock

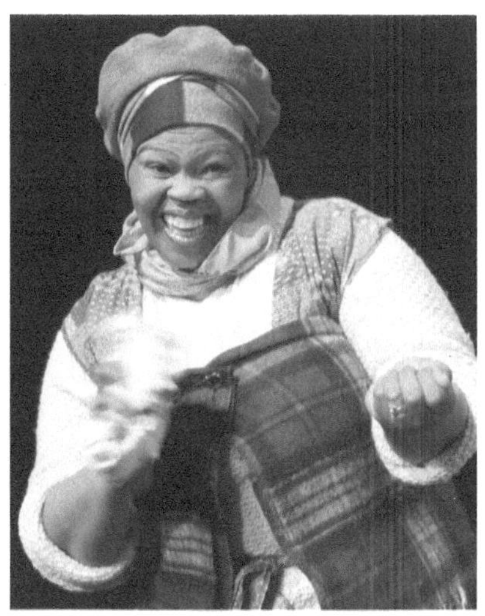

'Come here, my child, mntwana wam, you come to fetch a chicken for your mother.' 2006 © Ruphin Coudyzer

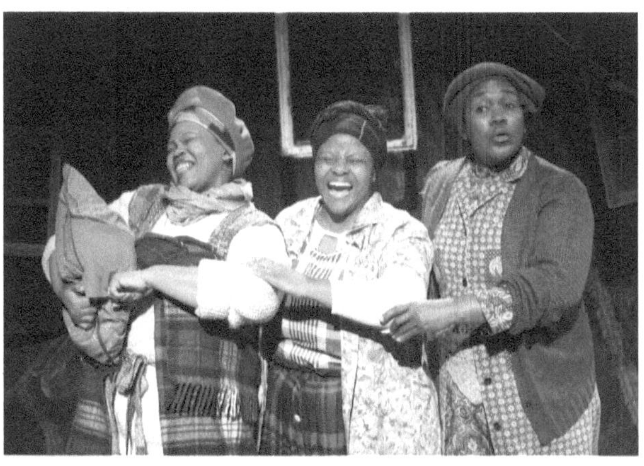

'Hamba kahle' . . . saying farewell to family and friends before boarding the bus from Transkei to Cape Town. 2006 © Ruphin Coudyzer

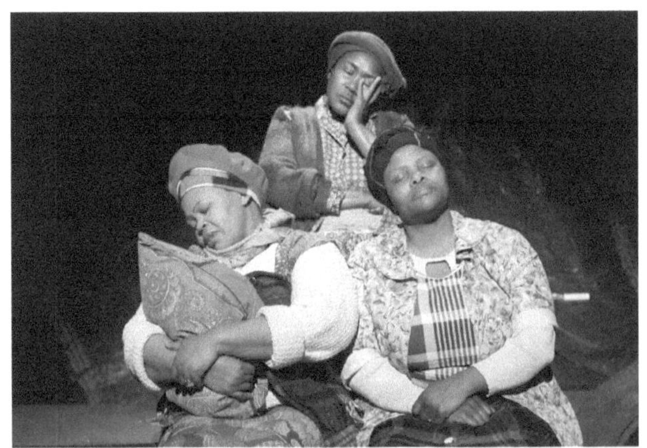

Sleeping on the bus. 2006 © Ruphin Coudyzer

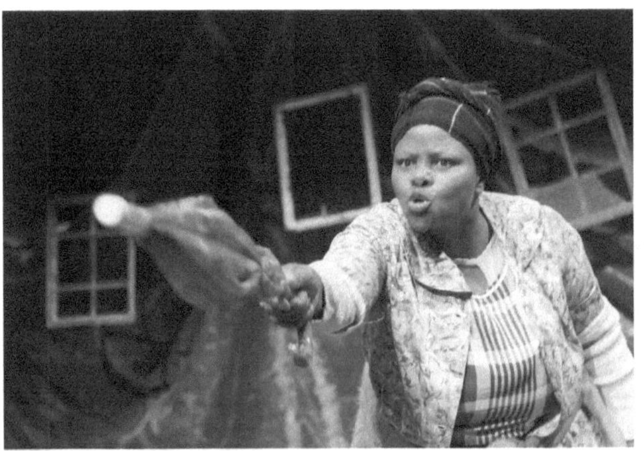

SDUDLA: 'Hey, what are you doing?' 2006 © Ruphin Coudyzer

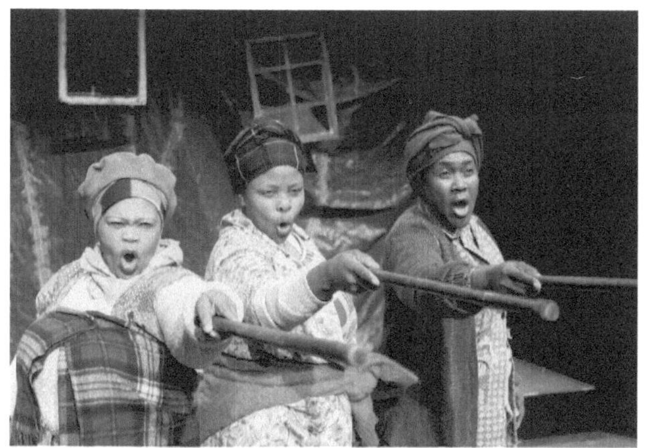

'Lenj' uBotha isiqhel' amasimba ngokubulalisa.' 2006 © Ruphin Coudyzer

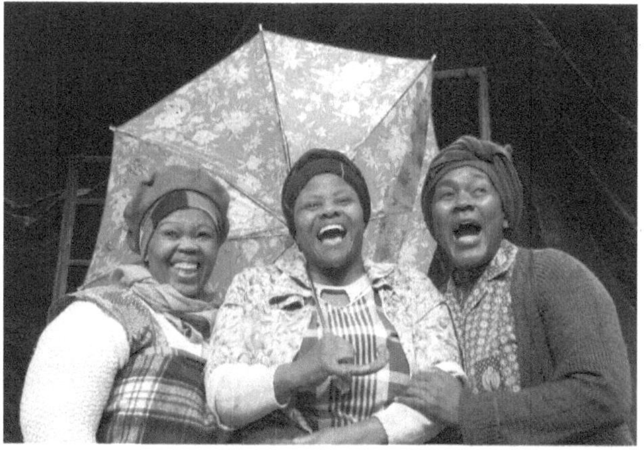

Smiling in the face of adversity. 2006 © Ruphin Coudyzer

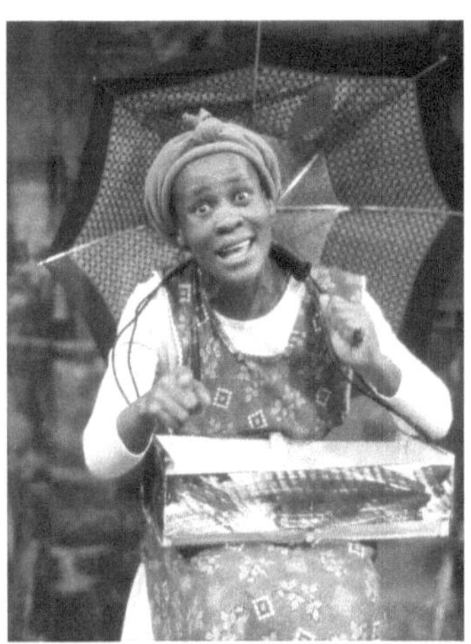

SDUDLA: 'So, if you want to go to heaven better get an orange.' 1987 © Ruphin Coudyzer

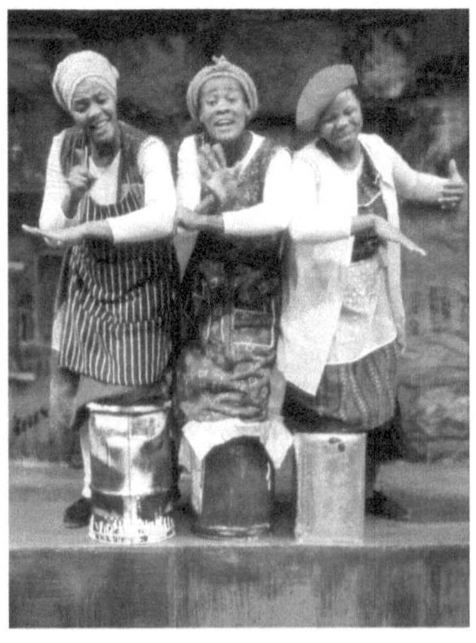

'Your mother is going to work in Cape Town for you.' 1987 © Ruphin Coudyzer

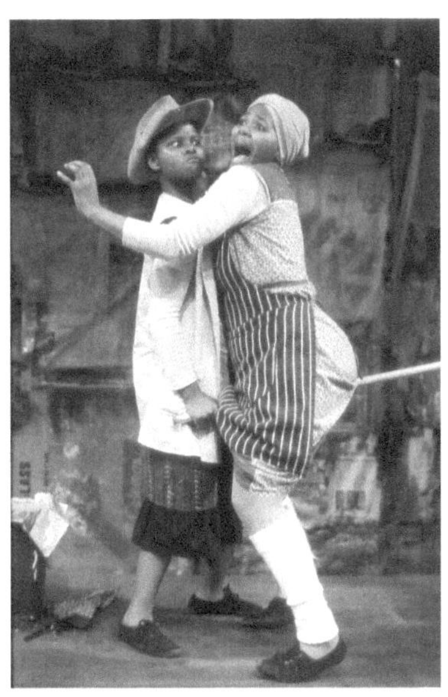

MAMBHELE as BOER to MAMPOMPO: 'Hands up!' 1987 © Ruphin Coudyzer

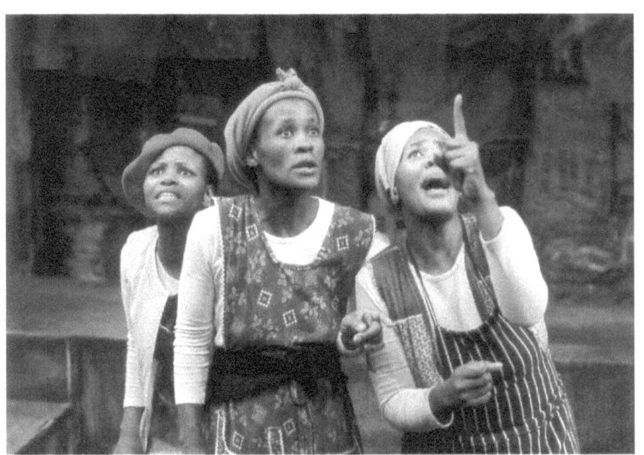

MAMBHELE: 'There is someone speaking from the bird in the sky.' 1987 © Ruphin Coudyzer

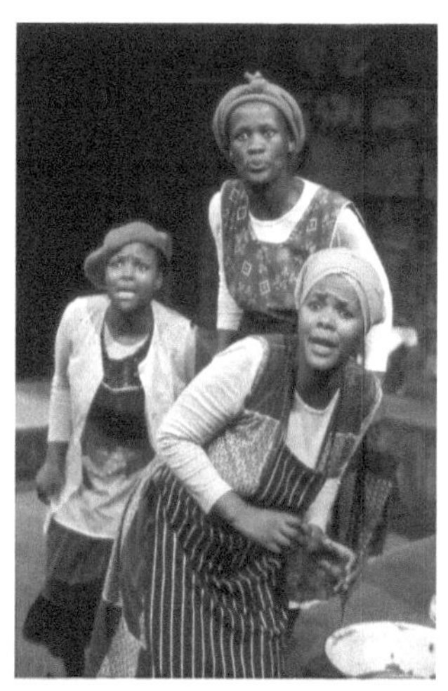

MAMPOMPO: 'Nazi! Nazi! A Hippo!' 1987 © Ruphin Coudyzer

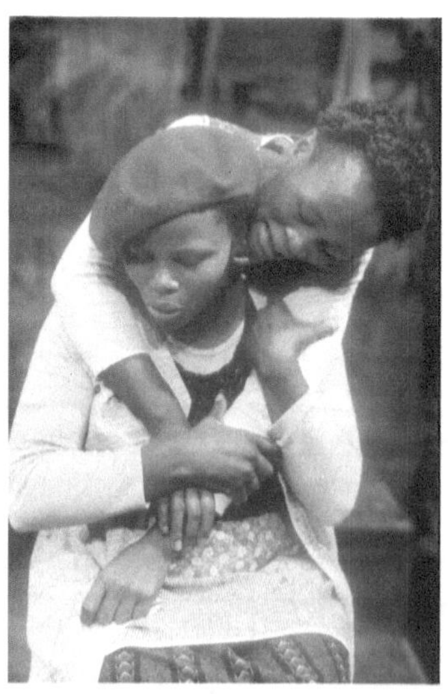

MAMBHELE: 'Your father was not always like this my child.' 1987 © Ruphin Coudyzer

You Strike A Woman, You Strike A Rock/Wathint' Abafazi, Wathint' Imbokotho

CHARACTERS

SDUDLA . . . A woman in her early 50s, highly politicised. She has suffered under the apartheid regime – her husband was arrested and taken away; her son fled into exile. These experiences have made her bitter and her behaviour is somewhat eccentric.

MAMPOMPO . . . A rural woman in her late 30s. She is gullible and believes the propaganda put out by the apartheid regime. Her main goal in life is to provide for her children.

MAMBHELE . . . A Cape Town woman in her late 30s. As a townswoman she is slightly more sophisticated than Mampompo and has developed risqué techniques to sell her chickens.

The many characters who people the market are visualised by the actors. Mampompo and Mambhele sell chickens. Sdudla sells oranges and vetkoek. Most of the props are mimed, except for the sticks. The actors play a variety of roles.

PRODUCTION HISTORY

The title of the play is taken from the slogan associated with the 1956 Women's March. Thirty years later we created a theatrical homage to the courage of our mothers. The play tells the personal stories of three women selling their wares in a township on the outskirts of Cape Town. It is a celebration of the spirit of millions of black women in South Africa who refused to give in to an oppressive system.

The play was first performed at the Arena Theatre, University of Cape Town, in May 1986, then at the Grahamstown Festival of the Arts on 29 June 1986 and later that year at the Baxter Studio Theatre, Cape Town, and the Market Theatre, Johannesburg, with Thobeka Maqhutyana, Poppy Tsira and Nomvula Qosha directed by Phyllis Klotz, stage manager Xolani September and set designer Sarah Roberts. The Community Arts Project and the Young People's Theatre Education Trust supported the production with financial assistance during the rehearsal period.

The play is set in a township marketplace, near a taxi rank. The non-realistic set suggests a wide open, dusty space. The action is played out against a triangular black plastic builder's sheet suspended from the ceiling. Behind the sheet hang three hessian panels of different sizes. Three rostra form a U – the upstage rostrum is twice the length of and a little higher than the other two. The rostra and floor are painted a muddy brown to give an earthy effect.

Four battered paraffin drums are scattered around the set. Each character has her own drum to use as she wishes. In addition, MAMPOMPO *has an enamel basin.* MAMBHELE *has two drums; one is covered with a wooden plank, the other she uses to mime dipping her chickens.*

PROLOGUE

A blue light placed centre stage swivels round and three shadowy figures run on stage making the sound of a helicopter. The three women huddle together centre stage continuing the sound of the helicopter. They focus on the light in fear, then split up and run in different directions, continuing the sound. SDUDLA *runs upstage on the rostrum,* MAMBHELE *downstage right,* MAMPOMPO *downstage left. A dim light comes up on* SDUDLA, *who is standing upstage centre.*

SDUDLA [*speaking over the sound of the helicopter*]: In the dead of the night there comes a plague bird . . .

MAMPOMPO: Hateful bird!

MAMBHELE: Ugly bird!

SDUDLA: . . . that runs above the location. The whistle blows, the people fear, mothers hush their children back to sleep, lock the doors. They creep, for that bird takes away our innocent sons and daughters. [*During the speech the helicopter light fades.*] At the heart of the location the bird lands. Quietness fills the whole location, weeping mothers protect their children as chickens protect their chicks from the hawk.

The sound of the helicopter breaks through and the women run around the stage looking for their children.

All is quiet.

SDUDLA [*anguished*]: Nyanisa, Nyanisa, Nyanisa, my child.

MAMBHELE: Titi, uphi? Titi, where are you?

MAMPOMPO: Mendo uphi na lo mntwana, Mendo uphi?

MAMBHELE: Hide, Titi. Come and hide, my child!

MAMPOMPO: Hide, Mendo. Hide, hide!

SDUDLA: Hide, Nyanisa, hide!

MAMPOMPO [*a cry*]: M-E-N-D-O!

SDUDLA: There was a full moon in the location. Knocking at the door was the man without pity. He took my child – when I gave birth to her I was happy for a moment when pains of labour arrived for I thought I was delivering a baby, but I wasn't. It was a victim of oppression.

MAMPOMPO *and* MAMBHELE *mime picking up stones to throw at the helicopter. The women begin to sing, pointing at the helicopter.*

ALL: Le ntaka, Ndizal' abantwana, Ndizal' amakhosi
Iya kufik' ibatshabalalise.

Blackout.

Scene 1

THE MARKETPLACE

Out of the dark comes the sound of a woman singing. A small pool of light fades up on MAMBHELE, *who is downstage, right at the edge of the rostra.*

MAMBHELE [*singing repeatedly and miming cleaning a chicken*]: Iinkuku zimnandi.

A small pool of light comes up on MAMPOMPO. *She is sitting on a tin drum downstage left, at the edge of the rostra.*

MAMPOMPO: The nice, big, fat, fresh chickens are here. Very cheap stuff. Woza mntwana.

MAMPOMPO *and* MAMBHELE *softly make the sound of chickens while* SDUDLA, *who is upstage centre sitting on her drum, shaded by a broken umbrella, half sings, half talks to her passing customers. Light slowly comes up on stage.*

SDUDLA: Oranges are cheap today, cheap today. Oranges are cheap today. So, if you want to go to heaven better get an orange. Hey [*to a particular customer*]! Buy an orange and suck it: the juice of this orange will open your eyes, you will know right from wrong.

MAMPOMPO *mimes a chicken running away from her. She runs after it across the stage, clucking like a chicken and shouting. She grabs the chicken by the neck and it wriggles in her hand.* MAMBHELE *laughs at her.*

MAMPOMPO [*turning to* MAMBHELE]: Uhleka ntoni? What are you laughing at, you bloody bitch? Le nkuku ibaleka nemali yabantwana bam. This chicken wants to run away – it is money. Ndiza kuyibulala. I'm going to kill it!

MAMBHELE: Since when do you know how to speak English?

MAMPOMPO: Hai! Shut up!

SDUDLA: Buy an orange before dying. [*She continues to sing her song.*]

MAMPOMPO [*calling to a passer-by*]: Yiza bhuti, chickens are cheap today. Nice, big, fat chickens, R5.50, R6.20, R7.20. Bhuti I'll give you two chickens. You can take one to your family in Transkei and you can eat the other one in the bus instead of eating mealies. Yiza bhuti, yiza.

MAMBHELE [*shaking her hand and blowing on it*]: I'm burning from the boiling water.

MAMPOMPO: Ah. The money is not burning – imali ayitshisi – you just take it and put in your pocket.

MAMBHELE [*suddenly spotting a customer*]: Heyi – ye Mqwathi, imali yam. The money from last month. My husband is also not working. You can't keep my money, you are not my bank.

MAMPOMPO [*speaking to the customer*]: Yee. Hey, since when do you buy chickens from her?

MAMBHELE: You are not funny! After all, you are working for Mrs Ntlebi. She exploits you. She does what she wants with you.

MAMPOMPO: I'm proud of it because I'm sure of my R2 a day, selling or not selling.

SDUDLA: Blessed are those who buy and see heaven right here. We all want to go to heaven but we don't want to die. Come buy and your eyes will be clear, you will make right what is wrong while still alive, don't wait after death – Woza mntwana – oranges, fat cakes. [*She continues to sing*]: Wanna go to heaven, better buy an orange.

MAMBHELE [*turning to an imaginary child*]: Come here, my child, mntwana wam, you came to fetch a chicken for your mother. I'll give you ibhasela of one chicken leg so that you can run home fast like Zola Budd.

SDUDLA [*seeing children in the distance*]: Ha! The children are coming back from school. Hey, what are you doing? [*She begins to wave her umbrella around wildly at the imaginary children, who are trying to take some of her oranges and fat cakes.*] So, they teach you to be thieves at school. What are you doing?

MAMPOMPO [*squatting over her enamel basin, trying to protect her chickens*]: These children are rude.

SDUDLA [*throwing her umbrella down, covering the box with her apron and shouting at the children*]: Voetsak! Fools! Hey, hey, thieves, you think I can't see you; if I get hold of you I'll give you what for.

MAMBHELE: What do you want? [*She shoos the children away.*] What do you want? Sdudla, leave them to have that orange.

MAMPOMPO: Sdudla, hit them with your umbrella.

MAMBHELE: Hayi, hayi, Sdudla, don't hit them with an umbrella, give them an orange.

MAMPOMPO: Why don't you give them one of your chickens?

MAMBHELE: The orange is small, the chicken is big.

SDUDLA: Hayi, voetsak! So they teach you to be thieves at school, maselandini. [*The two women begin to hum softly in the background:* Ntyilo, Ntyilo, *the sound of the birds.*] What do you expect, they teach them about thieves – those men from Europe, O Vasco da Gama and Jan van Riebeeck. They call me Aunty Sdudla and mock me. These, my children, mock me, they laugh – from the barrel of their bellies. These, my children – hoping my children's eyes will learn not dark alone; not foolishness, uselessness alone; not fear alone, because it is fear that ruins us and those who boss us take advantage of our fear and bully us forever; not hate alone – boss, boss – one day his boss called him a fool and the bloody boss hadn't even been to school. Then I close my eyes and hold my hat in my hand and hide my heart. [*The humming stops.*] To hell with boss, just call a spade a spade and kiss my black arse. Okay.

MAMPOMPO [*very excited, looking in the direction of the station*]: My dear, there are a lot of people coming from the station and the taxis are full.

MAMBHELE: My money! I'm waiting for my money, Mampompo, they are all drunk, they are coming from the shebeen.

MAMPOMPO: It's Friday today, business is like this [*makes a money sign*] and they are all drunk. They want something.

MAMBHELE *and* MAMPOMPO *turn to one another and hold out their hands.*

MAMPOMPO *and* MAMBHELE: Like food.

MAMPOMPO [*trying to attract customers*]: Bhuti yiza, the fat fresh chickens are here. The more chickens you eat the stronger you become, and you can make many children and girls will run after you.

MAMBHELE [*pointing to the customer*]: Hayi, that is my customer, he used to come to me every week, man.

MAMPOMPO: I didn't drag him, he just came.

MAMBHELE [*turning on all her charm and walking across the stage*]: Bhuti, bhuti, don't buy from her, she's a crook, she's got old chickens. Yiza bhuti. Come.

She puts her arm around the customer and walks off with him.

MAMPOMPO [*cross and slightly disdainful*]: You can have him. After all, he is the one who always touches you anyway. I don't like to sell my chickens to drunken men.

MAMBHELE [*sarcastically*]: This is the first I hear from you; you always sell your chickens to drunken men.

SDUDLA [*while she speaks the other two laugh at her and show that they don't take her ranting seriously*]: These, my children, in their kingdom switched on loud by liquor, drunk, petting girls on their buttocks, their kingdom which is ruled by the whistle, the call that tears into the dark like a sharp blade through a piece of cloth. [*She plays drunk.*] Hey, Aunty Sdudla, wanna see what God in heaven bought us this Friday? One bottle of brandy, one loaf of bread, one tin of pickled fish, two pounds ten to pay rent, what else . . . Bua. [*She bends over and pretends she is vomiting, making disgusting sounds.*]

MAMPOMPO [*running across the stage to attract the attention of her home boy*]: Tyhini molo Dlamini. How are you today? How's your family in the Transkei? Good, good, good. Yes, Dlamini, I'm still working here for Mrs Ntlebi. Hayi, hayi, Dlamini, you can't buy a chicken for R5.50 – since you have come from the Transkei you are stingy. You've got R10. [She *grabs the money out of his hand.*] I'll get you a big fat chicken. You see this big one, it's for you. Here's your change. Hayi, hayi, Dlamini, you can't complain about your change, R2.80 – you wanted a big chicken, it's R7.20.

MAMBHELE: You can't touch all my chickens and you are not buying. If you want to touch the thighs it's R2, the breast it's R5 and the whole chicken it's R15. [*She laughs, swivelling her hips.*] Nothing for nothing, everything is money. [*She sees a man she knows on the other side of the stage and waves to him.*] Awu Bhuti! You want a R6 chicken? Owu Bhuti, a big man like you [*pointing to his crutch*] who's big all over needs a big chicken. [*She walks along with the man, flirting. They stroll back to her drum, where she sees a child standing.*] My child [*rather sharply*], tell your mother I'll put a R6 chicken aside for her. Don't waste my time. [*A man comes up to her and pulls roughly at her breasts. She pretends to be shy.*] Hayi, Bhuti, don't hit my titties. Iyhuu, my money, Bhuti. [*He gives her the money and she puts it in her bra.*] I'll keep the change. See you next week Sunday [*waves goodbye*].

Throughout the above scene MAMPOMPO *has been watching* MAMBHELE *with obvious disgust.*

MAMPOMPO [*recognising the man*]: Hayi, hayi, you are my home boy – I know your wife. I'll tell her what's going on here. She'll take the clothes off your back. She is a Cape Town girl.

MAMBHELE [*laughs*]: That's how things are in the city. I'm not going to change them, I am going to pluck off his feathers.

MAMPOMPO: Ah? Are you going to pluck off his feathers?

MAMBHELE: Oh yes.

MAMPOMPO: Uthi uzakumxhutha?

MAMBHELE: Kakade.

MAMPOMPO: Since I came and worked here I noticed that all the men are touching you. You are selling the chickens and you are selling yourself.

MAMBHELE: It's none of your business.

MAMPOMPO: You call yourself a married woman – four children with four different fathers.

MAMBHELE: Who told you that I have four children with four different fathers? Nonsense!

MAMPOMPO: Let me tell you something. When I got married I was a virgin. I respect my husband and he respects me too.

MAMBHELE: Virgin or no virgin, we're all selling chickens.

MAMPOMPO: I've got four children from one father, not four children from four different fathers.

MAMBHELE: You think you're better, cheating the customers with change, stealing 5c to 10c a day.

The talk becomes more and more heated. MAMPOMPO *is very angry, obviously a nerve has been touched.*

MAMPOMPO: Have you seen it? Who told you that? Have you seen any of my customers complaining about the change? We Transkei people are hard workers.

MAMBHELE *begins to roll up her sleeves, obviously preparing for a fight.*

MAMPOMPO: You Cape Town people are lazy; you don't want to work.

MAMBHELE [*very angry*]: Who told you that?

The two women begin to push each other around. SDUDLA, *sitting on her tin drum underneath her umbrella, sees the police approaching. She makes the sound of a police siren. Immediately the women hear it they forget about their squabble and unite. They run to their chickens in an attempt to hide them from the police, as they haven't got a licence.*

MAMPOMPO: Owu Nkosi yam!

MAMBHELE: Iyawa ngala mapolisa.

MAMPOMPO [*angry*]: This Mrs Ntlebi doesn't want to pay a licence for me; if these police can come and take these chickens away she will deduct my money.

The siren becomes louder and the woman scramble around trying to collect their chickens.

MAMBHELE: Hayi, i-R50 yam imke namanzi, down the drain. We don't need them here. They should be protecting people whose houses are burning.

Holding her board she runs to hide and trips. MAMBHELE *and* MAMPOMPO *hide upstage behind the piece of sailcloth.*

SDUDLA [*sitting on her drum upstage centre and addressing the policeman with disdain*]: Heyi hamba, what are you doing here? What do you want? An orange? Give me 10c, I'll give you an orange so that the juice will open your eyes. Yes, I'm selling chickens too. A licence? Must I have a licence for oranges, a licence for chickens, a licence for fat cakes? Ag, you'll soon need a licence to go to the toilet and you'll call it a shit licence. Hamba sidenge – you fool.

The sounds of the van as the police drive off are made by the two hiding behind the sailcloth.

MAMBHELE [*emerging from behind the sailcloth*]: Nanga esiza nganeno la mapolisa.

SDUDLA: They were just passing. You were running around like your chickens when you're slaughtering them, you're lucky they didn't cut off your heads.

MAMPOMPO: Mambhele, I was shaking. I nearly made myself wet, my dear.

MAMBHELE [*laughing*]: He wethu, I was thinking that we were going to sleep in jail tonight.

MAMPOMPO: I didn't come to Cape Town to be a jailbird. I just came to Cape Town to work for my children.

MAMBHELE: Yhe wethu, they caught me one day. They took my chickens and money and I slept in jail that night. Another time they put me in a van and they drove around the location. Later they told me to go home.

MAMPOMPO: What about your chickens and money?

MAMBHELE: They took it. [*She points to* SDUDLA.] Is she not frightened of the police?

MAMPOMPO: Sdudla, aren't you afraid of them?

SDUDLA: If you check that big book at the police station my name is everywhere.

MAMPOMPO: I left Transkei, I came to Cape Town, same thing happens. There is no place for me. In Transkei we were starving, scratching for food and there was this terrible drought, cattle were dying and rivers were running dry and no jobs.

MAMBHELE: Where was your husband?

MAMPOMPO: He was here in Cape Town.

MAMBHELE: Why was he not helping you?

MAMPOMPO: He used to send us money. After some time he stopped doing so. Why? I don't know. [*She sits as she describes the scene.*] The first week of every month women are walking. Walking a long distance to the post office. Fat women, old women and pensioners, going to the post office to get some money from their husbands. Inside the post office, outside, the children are crying, women are pushing, they are all waiting for the money from those who are working in town.

Scene 2

THE POST OFFICE

MAMPOMPO: And there was this small window.

Light dims. She turns and knocks twice on the imaginary window upstage centre. SDUDLA, *as* OLD LADY, *enters, bumping* MAMPOMPO.

MAMPOMPO: She is supposed to be open now.

MAMBHELE *turns, changes into* PRETENTIOUS WOMAN *and joins the queue. The women queue, waiting for the post office to open, eyes fixed on the tiny window. They push and shove.*

MAMPOMPO: Molo. [*She waves and pushes backwards.*] Sontombi [*pushing forward*]. How are you today? Good. Good. Are you also coming for this? [*She indicates money.*] This is my fifth month now coming here. [OLD LADY *hits the person next to her.* MAMPOMPO *falls backwards.*] My fifth month – Mondays, Wednesdays, Fridays. I was very worried about my children. [*She faces the audience.*] What are they going to eat tonight?

PRETENTIOUS WOMAN *is pushed by* OLD LADY.

OLD LADY: Ah, it's very hot in here. I can't take it any longer. How long have you been here Noni sisi?

Both face forward, OLD LADY *trying to get air.*

MAMPOMPO: Long time I've been here, Granny.

OLD LADY: She should have opened by now.

MAMPOMPO: Who sends you money?

OLD LADY: Mm? I can't hear, my child.

MAMPOMPO: Who sends you money? Ngubani okuthumelela imali?

OLD LADY: My son.

MAMPOMPO: Where is your daughter-in-law?

OLD LADY: Mm?

MAMPOMPO: Where is your daughter-in-law? Uphi umolokazana wakho?

OLD LADY? UseKapa. She's in Cape Town with her husband. I'm looking after my two grandchildren. Please people, stop making this noise, otherwise I won't hear her footsteps when she is coming. You know [*she pushes to the right*], my son promised to send me money last month but I didn't get it, that's why I am here. [*She pushes* PRETENTIOUS WOMAN, *who is getting visibly angrier.*]

MAMPOMPO: Ahh.

Distracted, she turns to the window.

OLD LADY: I don't know what happened to him.

PRETENTIOUS WOMAN: How long must I stand here like a fool waiting for my money? Makhulu sukundiphusha. Don't push me! Five years ago I left you people like this and you're still the same. Nothing changes here in the Transkei.

She exits with a flourish.

OLD LADY [*waving her stick and watching her go*]: Hamba! Hamba!

MAMPOMPO [*watching* PRETENTIOUS WOMAN *exit*]: Hamba! She is rude.

She turns back to the window.

OLD LADY: You know, my son promised to send us money last month, but we didn't get it; that's why I am here. Last December when he came home he bought me a kist full of blankets and this shawl.

MAMPOMPO [*clearly not interested*]: It's very nice, Granny. [*She turns to the imaginary window.*]

OLD LADY [*touching her arm trying to get her attention and eventually pulling her sleeve*]: In December he came home with three 25lbs of sugar. I won't tell you how many tins of biscuits.

MAMPOMPO: Broken ones from the factory?

OLD LADY: Sweets, you know, the clothing for the children, three dresses for the girls, vests, a jacket for the boy.

POSTMISTRESS *played by* MAMBHELE *enters and opens the window, making the sound of window being opened.*

MAMPOMPO [*running to the window*]: I was the first one here.

OLD LADY [*pushing her with her elbow and knocking her away*]: Please, my child, don't push. Don't push.

MAMPOMPO: But Granny, you are the one who is pushing.

OLD LADY: I must stand in front, my child, otherwise I won't hear her when she is calling my name.

MAMPOMPO: I'm here since early this morning.

POSTMISTRESS: Thula! [*She waits for silence.*] Shut up!

MAMPOMPO: Stop pushing.

OLD LADY: I must stand in front.

MAMPOMPO: What's wrong with this old lady? What is your name?

OLD LADY: Thembela Mabhentsela.

POSTMISTRESS: I won't give you your money and letters. Keep quiet!

OLD LADY *continues to make a noise, improvising her dialogue as she goes on shouting at the other people to keep quiet. The* POSTMISTRESS *shows her full authority and behaves like a typical bureaucrat.* OLD LADY *realises that she will only call the names when there is quiet. Silence.* POSTMISTRESS *begins to call out names.*

POSTMISTRESS: Nomaliza Kakwana, Thandiwe Sigebenga. [OLD LADY *and* MAMPOMPO *follow the women getting their money and signing for it.*] Ngubani . . . [MAMPOMPO *makes the sound of a baby crying.*] umama walo mntwana? This child must keep quiet. [*The baby quietens down.*]

Silence. MAMPOMPO *and the* OLD LADY *huddle together and smile at the* POSTMISTRESS.

POSTMISTRESS: Thembela Mabhentsela. Thembela Mabhentsela.

OLD LADY [*starts talking as soon as the* POSTMISTRESS *begins to call out names*]: Shut up! I won't hear her when she's calling my name.

MAMPOMPO: Granny, she is calling your name.

OLD LADY: Thembela Mabhentsela. It's me, sana wam.

POSTMISTRESS: Granny, I've been calling your name for a long time.

OLD LADY: I've been trying to get through this crowd, my child.

POSTMISTRESS: Here you are, Granny. Sign.

OLD LADY: I can't write, my child.

POSTMISTRESS: Give me your thumb. Registered letter, money, Makhulu. Open a space for her.

> OLD LADY *exits, waving the envelope with the money and singing a hymn,* 'Nkosi yam'.

POSTMISTRESS [*continues calling out names*]: Nomabhisiniya Ndlebe, Mgothovu Ngcondo.

> POSTMISTRESS *closes the window, making the sound of the window closing, then mimes having a cup of tea.* MAMPOMPO *knocks on the window, making the sound nkqo, nkqo . . . She becomes very distressed. The* POSTMISTRESS *continues to drink her tea slowly, then puts down the cup and opens the window, once again making the sound of the window opening.*

POSTMISTRESS: What is the matter?

MAMPOMPO: You didn't call my name.

POSTMISTRESS: I know your name, you are always here.
MAMPOMPO: Please check again. Check.
POSTMISTRESS: Yes, if it's not here, it's not here.

She closes the window rapidly.

MAMPOMPO *knocks repeatedly, but to no avail. Her knocks get slower and softer and she stands alone in a pool of light, which slowly fades.*

Scene 3

THE BUS

MAMPOMPO: Nkqonkqoza.

Lights come up slowly as MAMBHELE *enters.*

MAMBHELE: Nkqo, Nkqo, Nkqo . . . Yintoni mntase.

MAMPOMPO: I decided to go to Cape Town. I took my four children to my mother.

MAMBHELE: Where did you get the money from?

MAMPOMPO: I got R50 from cutting and selling bundles of grass. From that money I bought a bus ticket, my dear.

General noise as the actors pick up drums and put them on their heads. They move downstage right and mime leaning out of the windows of a bus. They are in a pool of light. The rest of the stage is dimly lit.

DOMESTIC WORKER [*played by* SDUDLA]: Lungiswa, Lungiswa, come quickly, the bus is going to move.

YOUNG MOTHER [*played by* MAMBHELE]: Nomathamsanqa, bring that bag with the nappies.

MAMPOMPO: Nomqondiso, hurry up! Bring my coolbag. Yiza naloo my coolbag. Where are the other children? Sqosho, move, the bus is leaving.

DOMESTIC WORKER: Sapha, my blanket, maan, my blanket.

YOUNG MOTHER: Sapha loo bhotile yomntwana. Bring that bottle.

MAMPOMPO: Sapha lo coolbag. Nomqondiso, help your granny fetch some water before you go to school and when you come from school, my child.

DOMESTIC WORKER: Yha Lungiswa, I'll go and see your brother in Pollsmoor prison and give him the message about your mother. Ah! Don't worry, I'll ask permission for him to attend the funeral.

YOUNG MOTHER: You've got the new address and the phone number. You must come and visit us.

MAMPOMPO: Sqosho, please don't forget to count the sheep every evening. They must be the same number my son.

YOUNG MOTHER: I know the life in Transkei is very bad. When is your husband's contract finished on the gold mine?

DOMESTIC WORKER: Lungiswa, I'll write. Don't forget to answer.

YOUNG MOTHER: Save money and come to us.

MAMPOMPO: Sqosho, don't forget to milk the cow every morning, otherwise you'll starve. Uyakudliwa yindlala mntan' am.

YOUNG MOTHER: She looks like her father, unguyise esinya when he is shitting on the toilet.

MAMPOMPO: Nomqondiso, please bantwana bam, don't fight over nothing. Attend school every day. Your mother is going to work in Cape Town for you. I'll send you clothing.

YOUNG MOTHER: You mean the father of this child? I don't know where he is. I've been looking for him everywhere – the prisons, hospitals. His comrade said he was taken away.

DOMESTIC WORKER: Oh please, Lungiswa, don't forget to keep an eye on my mother, and see that my child is attending school.

MAMPOMPO: Please, my children, don't cry. Sanukulila. Sqosho, do you remember those football boots you wanted? It will be 1, 2, 3, and your mother will send them to you. Your mother is going to work in Cape Town, my son. Bye bye bantwana bam.

DOMESTIC WORKER [*waving frantically*]: Bye bye, Lungiswa. Bye bye. I will write. I will write, next year, next year. [*She laughs.*]

The lights dim. The women turn in slow motion towards stage left. They wave and turn their backs. As they face the audience again they become the characters who came to the bus to say goodbye to their relatives. MAMPOMPO *becomes the child she was talking to.* DOMESTIC WORKER *becomes her cousin.* YOUNG MOTHER *becomes her friend. The actors need to make these character changes very clear.*

CHILD: Mama, mama, don't forget my football boots.

FRIEND: Hamba kahle. Farewell.

COUSIN: The funeral, the funeral. Your brother in Pollsmoor, Pollsmoor prison.

CHILD [*crying*]: Mama . . . Mama!

The actors make the sound of the bus as they move across the stage, collect their drums and place them centre stage. MAMPOMPO *sits on a drum on a higher rostrum with two drums in front of her. The others sit on the drums, giving the effect of sitting on a bus.* DOMESTIC WORKER *is next to the window on the right. When they are all seated they stop making the sound of the bus and mime the movement.*

MAMPOMPO [*wiping away her tears*]: It's not easy to leave the children like this, but what can I do?

The YOUNG MOTHER *holds her baby in her arms, bouncing it up and down. The* DOMESTIC WORKER *leans over to the baby, making cooing sounds and playing with her.*

MAMPOMPO [*waving her hand around in the air as though there is smoke blowing in her face*]: Old man, please stop smoking. I've got a terrible headache. Tata sukutshaya, intloko yam iyaqaqamba. [*She leans forward and opens the window.*]

DOMESTIC WORKER [*reading a magazine, starts to feel the draught and looks up*]: Excuse me lady, did you open the window on purpose? [*She stresses* purpose.]

MAMPOMPO: Yes, my child, I have a terrible headache.

YOUNG MOTHER: Aunty, close the window, the draught is on my baby.

MAMPOMPO [*pointing to her head indicating she has a headache*]: Hayi, hayi, mntan'am intloko yam iyaqaqamba.

DOMESTIC WORKER *shuts the window firmly.*

YOUNG MOTHER: Thank you.

Silence. The actors continue with the motion of the bus throughout the scene. The DOMESTIC WORKER *and the* YOUNG MOTHER *indicate they are about to fall asleep. We hear the sounds of Radio Xhosa.* DOMESTIC WORKER *and* YOUNG MOTHER *start singing the words of an advertisement, as if they are the voices coming from the radio.*

DOMESTIC WORKER *and* YOUNG MOTHER: Wilsons Extra Strong . . .

MAMPOMPO [*addressing a passenger*]: Toto, you can play your wireless if you can play it softer. [*The sound fades and she relaxes.*] That's the way. [*As she gets comfortable the sound is turned up. She is furious.*] Hayi, hayi, switch off that wireless, people want to sleep. [*The radio is turned off.*] Ndakunyisa!

The YOUNG MOTHER *falls asleep, as does the* DOMESTIC WORKER, *who begins to snore.* MAMPOMPO *watches them for a while, then quickly opens the window. The* DOMESTIC WORKER, *feeling the draught in her sleep, reacts. She opens her eyes and, obviously annoyed, stands up and closes the window.*

MAMPOMPO [*opening it*]: Ndiyayivula.

DOMESTIC WORKER [*closing it*]: Ndiyayivala.

MAMPOMPO [*opening it*]: Ndiyayivula.

DOMESTIC WORKER [*slamming it shut*]: Ndiyayivala. Name, Okwakho.

Silence once more. Everyone settles down to sleep. The YOUNG MOTHER *makes the sound of her baby crying.*

DOMESTIC WORKER: Why do you have to sleep while your baby is crying? Feed your baby!

MAMPOMPO [*leaning over and gesturing, points to her breast*]: Makoti ncancisa umntwana. Feed your baby. These youngsters like to have babies but they don't know how to look after them.

The YOUNG MOTHER *mimes taking out her breast to feed the baby.* She *puts the baby to the breast but from the sounds it makes it is obvious that it doesn't want to be fed. The mother thinks that perhaps the baby has messed in its nappy and begins to investigate. Indicating that the nappy smells bad she starts to change it. The* DOMESTIC WORKER *smells something, turns in the direction of the smell and becomes very angry.*

DOMESTIC WORKER: Makoti, you don't have to change a shit nappy in the bus!

YOUNG MOTHER [*throwing the soiled nappy on the floor, causing the* DOMESTIC WORKER *to move her legs sharply out of the way*]: Must I keep my baby with one nappy from Transkei to Cape Town?

DOMESTIC WORKER: Why didn't you ask the driver to stop the bus?

YOUNG MOTHER: Only for a nappy?

MAMPOMPO [*who has been eating a sandwich*]: Hayi, this is too much. I'm busy eating while you are changing a shit nappy. I've got no appetite anymore.

DOMESTIC WORKER *opens the window and leans out, gasping for fresh air.*

MAMPOMPO: I told you a long time ago to open the window. Can you see now? You think you are clever.

Pause.

MAMPOMPO: How far are we?

DOMESTIC WORKER: A long way.

MAMPOMPO: Have you been to Cape Town?

DOMESTIC WORKER: Yes, I've been working there for six years.

MAMPOMPO: Six years! I'm going to my husband. Here is his address.

DOMESTIC WORKER: Show the driver. Well, sisi, it's still a lot of time to go, hlala phantsi. Sit down. [*She goes to sleep.*]

Baby cries – bus stops. The DOMESTIC WORKER *and the* YOUNG MOTHER *turn to look at* MAMPOMPO *and whisper.*

YOUNG MOTHER: It seems as if she doesn't have a permit for Cape Town.

MAMPOMPO [*left alone, prays*]: Oh God, don't let them stop the bus. I must go to Cape Town and look for my husband, and work for my children.

Scene 4

THE DOMPAS

Lights up to general.

SDUDLA: You came to Cape Town thinking that all your problems would be solved.

MAMPOMPO: Yes, especially now because Botha has taken the passes away so that I can go wherever I want to.

SDUDLA: Ha! People say I am mad. I never took a dompas, from when it started until now when President Botha says it's over.

MAMBHELE: That Botha has been promising everyone everything.

MAMPOMPO: Ha. You are born in Cape Town, you've got all the rights; you've got a pass, unepasi wena.

MAMBHELE: If everything was like you say I wouldn't be here with all my section 10s, a, b, c, up to z permits and my pass.

MAMPOMPO: Heyi mfazi, is Sdudla like me, not having a permit or a pass?

SDUDLA: Never, ever in my life, kaloku mfazi.

MAMBHELE: You are like children to that Botha, because he's telling you fairy tales.

MAMPOMPO: You can say anything about him, I won't listen because he's good to me.

MAMBHELE: He is so tricky. Every day we read in the papers, we listen to the radio that things are changing, but nobody knows what is going on. Do you think that Botha is going to let us do anything, go anywhere, stay anywhere without a permit? They are going to control us. Inkom' ingazala umntu. You will wait and wait until your eyes are grey.

SDUDLA: Mampompo, if they say the pass is finished why do they say people must keep their passes? Why? Because they are frightened that the women will start burning their passes as they did 30 years ago. What will they do then?

MAMPOMPO: Hayi suka, you Cape Town people say all these things as an excuse not to work. What kind of work do you want to do? I can take any work – domestic . . . I even worked on a farm. When I came to Cape Town my husband was in hospital with TB. His brother took me to the hospital but they didn't want me to see him because he was so sick. His brother took me back to the hostel. As you know I was not allowed to stay there because of my permit. He took me to Crossroads, where we can build a shack. But I didn't even have money to build a shack. I stayed with people. I can take any work to make money. You [*referring to* MAMBHELE] are choosy, fussy and lazy.

MAMBHELE: Choosy, fussy, lazy! Since you come from Transkei you think you are clever and your eyes are wide open. If you think your eyes are wide open why don't you see things that are happening around you? Hey? Let me tell you where I come from. You just see me here in this marketplace. If I should tell you about places that I've worked at I would talk for the whole day. Rha mnqundu wakho, qabakazi ndini. Does a lazy person wake up in the morning, catch the earliest train, run like mad dogs to the station?

Scene 5

THE TRAIN

As the lights fade SDUDLA *crosses to* MAMPOMPO, *who is sitting on her drum. Both play domestic workers on their way to work early in the morning.* SDUDLA *plays* COMMUTER 1 *and* MAMPOMPO COMMUTER 2.

COMMUTER 1 [*standing behind* MAMPOMPO *and pointing to* COMMUTER 2*'s watch*]: What time is it?

COMMUTER 2: Heyi mfazi, we are late. We must run, otherwise we will miss the train.

They begin to run upstage. MAMBHELE *remains downstage centre.*

COMMUTER 1: Late, late, something to six.

MAMBHELE: Where is my ticket? I haven't got extra money to buy another one.

COMMUTER 2: Which platform is the next train?

COMMUTER 1: Platform 4.

MAMBHELE: Where is my ticket? In my jersey?

COMMUTER 2 [*stops to catch her breath*]: Yhu! Running like this while master and madam are still playing hide and seek in bed.

COMMUTER 1: You mean you didn't finish yours?

COMMUTER 2: There is no time for that, man, I'm too tired. Him too.

They stand waiting for the train and then make the sound of the train stopping.

MAMBHELE: Thank God, I found it.

The women rush into the train, bumping and pushing one another, searching for a seat. COMMUTER 1 *sits down.* MAMBHELE *brushes past her.*

COMMUTER 1: Don't stick your stinking bum in my face.

MAMPOMPO *stands as though holding onto a rail and almost falls as the train pulls out of the station. The women mime the motion of the train.*

COMMUTER 2: I am worried because I am leaving my children alone and I don't know what I'm going to find when I get back from work.

COMMUTER 1: My eldest is giving me trouble. He doesn't want to go to school; makes trouble with the other children while I am at work.

COMMUTER 2: These days I can't go to work and leave my children at home and feel peace.

MAMBHELE: Women, let us take our troubles to Jesus the Saviour, he is always with us. Let us praise the Lord this morning for saving us.

COMMUTER 2: Jesus!

MAMBHELE: And for being with us up to now. Let us pray and ask God to keep His eyes on our homes.

COMMUTER 1: Glory to God.

MAMBHELE: Oh Jesus, look after our children . . .

COMMUTER 2: Jesus!

MAMBHELE: While some of us are going to look after our madams' homes and children . . .

COMMUTERS 1 *and* 2: Hallelujah!

MAMBHELE: Our homes are painted red; painted by the blood of our children, for when the day comes we shall enter the Kingdom of Heaven.

ALL TOGETHER: Oh Lord, spread your wings and protect our children while we are at work.

MAMBHELE [*singing*]: We thank you our Lord.

We thank you Jesus
Uzusithethelele Baba
Uzusithethelele Jesu
Uzusithethelele

CHORUS: Hallelujah!

The actors go from the scene on the train directly into the following scene, maintaining the rhythm of the train.

Scene 6

THE WORKPLACE

TOGETHER [*in the rhythm of a train*]: Chook-chook-chook-WORK
Chook-chook-chook-WORK
Chook-chook-chook-WORK

CHORUS: Work-work, work-work-work;
Work-work, work-work-work;
Work-work, work-work-work;
Work-work, work-work-work.

MAMPOMPO [*walking across the stage as* MADAM]: Oh Florence, late for work again! I really can't have this, you know. You are unreliable – either you are late or you have got some weak excuse for taking days off and then you expect to be paid. I think it best you leave.

MAMBHELE: Madam, I had to take my child to the clinic, the doctor doesn't know what is the matter with her.

MADAM: You must understand that I work as well and I simply can't have someone who is unreliable. Who will be here when my children come home from school? I never know where I am with you, Florence. I'll give you your money and you must go.

TOGETHER: Chook-chook-chook-WORK
Chook-chook-chook-WORK
Chook-chook-chook-WORK

Lights change.

SDUDLA [*as* SUPERVISOR]: Listen, sisi, if you want a contract as a cleaner in an office building . . .

ALL TOGETHER: Work!

SUPERVISOR: . . . you must be prepared to work the early morning shift.

ALL TOGETHER: Work!

SUPERVISOR: You will have one floor to clean; five toilets.

MAMBHELE: The toilets are so big a family could live in them. Two kitchens bigger than my whole house.

SUPERVISOR: You must start with emptying the dustbins and ashtrays, then dust, even the pictures on the wall.

ALL TOGETHER: Work!

SUPERVISOR: The pay is R70 a week.

ALL TOGETHER: Work!

SUPERVISOR: Do you want the job?

MAMBHELE: What can I say? I need the money. I can't refuse the work.

ALL TOGETHER: Work! Work! Work! Work!

The actors begin to mime various activities in a laundry to a regular rhythmical count of four. SDUDLA *is ironing sheets,* MAMPOMPO *is sorting washing into trolleys and* MAMBHELE *is working with a heavy pressing machine. All their actions are stylised. They make a sound expelling air to co-ordinate with downward movements. The rhythm continues throughout the sequence.*

MAMPOMPO *and* SDUDLA: Work, work, work, work.

MAMBHELE: I was pleased to get this job at the laundry.

MAMPOMPO *and* SDUDLA [*speeding up the rhythm*]: Work, work, work, work.

MAMBHELE: Regular hours, no night shift.

MAMPOMPO *and* SDUDLA: Work, work, work, work.

MAMBHELE: I could be at home with my children, and the money was alright.

MAMPOMPO *and* SDUDLA: Work, work, work, work.

Rhythm and action continue.

MAMBHELE: The machine was heavy and I had to stand on my feet for long hours.

MAMPOMPO *and* SDUDLA: Work, work, work, work.

MAMBHELE: But I didn't worry . . .

MAMPOMPO *and* SDUDLA: Work, work, work, work.

MAMBHELE: What I didn't know was that I was pregnant.

MAMPOMPO *and* SDUDLA: Work, work, work, work.

MAMBHELE: I began to get cramps in my stomach and bleed. I had a miscarriage.

MAMPOMPO *and* SDUDLA: Work, work, work, work.

MAMBHELE: I stayed away from work for three days . . .

MAMPOMPO *and* SDUDLA: Work, work, work, work.

MAMBHELE: When I went back the boss said to me . . .

MAMPOMPO [*as* BOSS, *pointing a finger*]: I don't think you are serious about your work.

MAMPOMPO *and* SDUDLA: Work, work, work, work.

BOSS: You are already taking days off.

MAMPOMPO *and* SDUDLA: Work, work, work, work.

BOSS: You are fired.

ALL TOGETHER: Work, work, work, work. [*They get back on the train.*] Chook, chook, chook, chook.

SDUDLA [*hymn sung quietly under the sound of the train*]: Oh Jesus, spread your wings and protect our children while we are at work, so that when we come home late at night or early in the evening we may find them safe.

They all sing a Church of Zion hymn in joyful exaltation. MAMBHELE *drums on the rostrum, beating time.*

ALL TOGETHER: Ozayo Makabongwe
Hosannah in the highest
Let him be praised.

CHORUS: Hallelujah!

COMMUTER 2: Jesus – Amen.

Blackout.

Scene 7

THE FARM

SDUDLA *is singing the hymn softly as the lights go up.*

SDUDLA: Hey, buy an orange and the juice will open your eyes.

MAMPOMPO [*looking around downstage*]: Where are the people today? It's getting late. I must sell more chickens, otherwise Mrs Ntlebi will give me the sack.

MAMBHELE: Why don't you sell your chickens on credit?

MAMPOMPO: Hayi, hayi, Mambhele, you know Mrs Ntlebi won't allow me to do that.

MAMBHELE: Mampompo, can't you see that there are green flies on your chickens?

SDUDLA: Hayi, it's because your chickens are very expensive, nobody wants to buy them.

MAMPOMPO: Sdudla, do you remember that day Mrs Ntlebi came here and shouted at me because I didn't sell enough chickens?

MAMBHELE: That one, she does what she wants with you, pays you R2 a day. Have you seen the smart car she bought herself? While you stand working here in the rain and sun, she is driving in it. What is this bonus business you are talking about?

MAMPOMPO: If I sell a lot of chickens she gives me an extra 20 cents for every chicken.

MAMBHELE: How many extra chickens?

MAMPOMPO: That depends on how she is feeling.

MAMBHELE: Now you know why I am my own boss.

MAMPOMPO: I can't afford that. At least I'm sure of my R2 a day. You don't know how much you are going to get and sometimes you sell very little, just like today.

SDUDLA *starts making the sound of a helicopter.* MAMBHELE *and* MAMPOMPO *join in. They mime as if it is flying overhead and duck as it goes past.*

SDUDLA: There must be trouble somewhere, that bird has been flying over us all day.

MAMPOMPO: Don't let it come here, let it happen in the other townships. Mrs Ntlebi will deduct money from me if anything happens to her chickens.

MAMBHELE: People say her house in the township is beautiful – just like a white person's. Why don't you leave her?

MAMPOMPO: Shit, it's nice working here. I'm even used to this brutal murder. I even dream about the sound of chickens.

SDUDLA [*makes the sound of chickens, making fun of the other two*]: Chickens, chickens.

MAMPOMPO: Thula, Sdudla. Thula, Sdudla.

MAMBHELE: She is starting again.

MAMPOMPO: Sdudla, go and sell somewhere else. I'm sick and tired of your nonsense. Oh God – today it's this, tomorrow it's another thing. What was I saying?

MAMBHELE: We were talking about your job.

MAMPOMPO: Oh this job! It's better than the other jobs I had, working for a family day and night for little pay. The only thing that was better was that my stomach was full. Madam was always shouting and saying I was breaking her things.

SDUDLA [*imitating employer*]: 'You break my vase, a present from my mother!'

MAMPOMPO: She is bad – she is getting worse every day. That madam, she told me to go. The worst job I ever had was on a farm in Philippi. It wasn't the hard work that I hated, but this other business.

Exit MAMBHELE.

SDUDLA *and* MAMPOMPO [*playing farmworkers and singing*]:

Iyhoho sotshona phin' amadoda. Halala!
Sotshona phin' amadoda?
Iyhoho sotshona phin' amadoda?
Abantwana bethu sebelala ngendlala.
Halala sotshona phin' amadoda?
Where is our hideout? My children are sleeping with hunger.

MAMBHELE *enters as the* BOER. *She wears a farmer's hat, carries a large stick and speaks in Afrikaans. During the song the* BOER *picks his teeth to amuse himself.*

BOER: Dis al tyd om huis toe gaan – kom, kom! [*The two women hesitate.*] Come here at once!

MAMPOMPO *goes to the* BOER, *who is standing on the back rostrum. He begins to search her, rubbing her breast and patting her backside.*

BOER [*slapping her backside*]: Nice and fat.

MAMPOMPO *walks away, muttering as she goes in frustration and anger. The other woman goes up to him and he begins to search her. The* BOER *hears* MAMPOMPO *and pushes the other woman aside.*

BOER [*to* MAMPOMPO, *beckoning*]: Come here. I'm the boss. [MAMPOMPO *goes to him and he pushes her legs open with his stick.*] Hands up!

She does as he says. He slowly takes the stick and begins to use it in a sexually abusive manner. He pulls her towards him and then violently pushes her aside. MAMPOMPO *feels violated.*

MAMPOMPO [*aggressively*]: Tlola, ngwana re bone blumas.

SDUDLA [*in time to the song* 'Jump, child, so we see the panties', *a song sung to the tune of one of the cultural play songs that girls sing*]: Rha! You dog. [*She continues with the song.*] Tlola, ngwana re bone blumas.

MAMPOMPO: Rha! You with your small prick. You can't even get it up.

The women sing together defiantly at the BOER, *who has turned his back. They sing the song three times: on the second-last word of the last line they lift their skirts to match his uncouth behaviour.* BOER *exits.* MAMPOMPO *returns to her story.*

MAMPOMPO: Sometimes he didn't want to give us our wages – R14 a week – he gave us potatoes and a few carrots.

Scene 8

THE SYSTEM

MAMBHELE: I wouldn't stay at that job. Yaw, men think we are toys for them to play with. No, no! That's why I told my husband to go, but he doesn't want to.

SDUDLA: These men think they can control us. I remember attending meetings a long time ago where men stood up and said that the government could not give us black women passes because that woman is under the control of a man. They thought we would not listen to them anymore.

MAMPOMPO: Ja, the man is the head of the house, you do what he says – it is our tradition.

MAMBHELE: You people from Transkei are old fashioned. Aren't we working hard, earning the money to support our children? Must we still do what they say?

SDUDLA: Mampompo, for years now we black women have been fighting for our rights. It is a long, hard struggle. We are treated like children by everyone, but as wives and mothers it falls upon us to make small wages stretch a long way. It is we who feel the cries of our children when they are sick and hungry. It suits the men to keep us like fools.

MAMPOMPO: Sdudla, you are mad! There must be something wrong with you upstairs. You have never taken a pass, always working here in this place, and now you want me to tell my husband what to do . . . Hayi uyandinyela. You are shitting on me.

MAMBHELE: Everyone is telling you what to do – your madam, the Boer, your black boss, your husband . . . when are you going to do something by yourself?

MAMPOMPO: Nonsense! I told myself to come to Cape Town. If I don't like a job I can leave.

SDUDLA: What job can you get? [*No answer.*] Mampompo? You see you are qualified for nothing and you will do what others tell you your whole life.

MAMBHELE [*to a customer*]: Mamqwambi mfazi, you know very well I don't give credit near the end of the month. No, I can't hear about problems. Everybody living under this system has got problems. You still owe me money from last month. If you give me the money you will get a chicken. [*Sarcastically*] You think I can give you another?

MAMPOMPO [*looking around*]: There are few people here today. Hey! Why must these children come and play football here? Hamba, you are making dust on my chickens, now I must cover them with a cloth.

SDUDLA: Voetsek! So you think I can't see you, children brought up without the proper care of their mothers; fathers who leave home for work and sometimes never come back; mothers too tired to talk to you or know you.

MAMPOMPO: Hey, hey, are you answering me back? I'll give you a hot klap.

MAMBHELE: Where do you think these children can go and play? There is nowhere else for them.

SDUDLA: Sdudla, Sdudla, chicken legs. Little fools! Who are you mocking? Have we been struggling all these years for you to laugh at us? We have given birth to a nation of children who think the struggle started with them. They know nothing of their history because it is hidden from them in their schools.

MAMBHELE [*laughs*]: Are you going to lecture them on their hidden history? [*She continues to laugh.*]

SDUDLA: Laugh, laugh, you can laugh. The men laughed at us in 1956. They thought we would not make it, but we showed them. Laugh! What do you know about our mothers who founded the Federation of South African Women – Dora Tamana, Annie Silinga, Lilian Ngoyi? The road to freedom is a long one, with many hills to climb. Now I remember, I was a girl of 18. It was 1956 when we marched to Pretoria to protest against the pass laws.

MAMBHELE *and* MAMPOMPO [*singing and the lights fade*]:

Baphin' ooSilinga
Baphin' ooTamana

MAMBHELE: Women rose up together and the numbers swelled like a great wave in the ocean.

MAMPOMPO: United they went to face the prime minister, Strijdom.

The song continues. SDUDLA *stands above the back rostrum.*

SDUDLA: I put my baby on my back and we went to Pretoria. We couldn't get transport. The government made it difficult for us but we didn't care. We didn't have anywhere to leave our children, so we took them with us. We went by foot . . . bus . . . train to Pretoria. When we got near Pretoria we heard that the meeting had been banned, but that didn't worry us – we went in twos and threes until we reached the Union Buildings.

MAMPOMPO *and* MAMBHELE [*singing*]:

Baphin' ooSilinga
Baphin' ooTamana
Singene Enkululekweni
Till we have our freedom.

SDUDLA: There were thousands of us – standing everywhere . . . on the steps, in the big space before the buildings. Black women in traditional dresses, white women, Indian women in white saris. Hey! Some of us brought our madams' children. We left our protest forms, then we stood in silence for half an hour. After that we sang the anthem, and then we went home with our babies on our backs.

ALL TOGETHER [*singing*]:

Lo Mzabalazo
Sonyuka nawo
Singene Enkululekweni.

SDUDLA: After that I was married to my husband. One night I saw a man in blue pass by our window.

MAMPOMPO *as* POLICEMAN 1 [*stamping foot*]: Open up!

MAMBHELE *as* POLICEMAN 2 [*stamping foot*]: Open up!

SDUDLA: Who the hell is open up?

POLICEMEN [*together*]: As if you didn't hear . . . Open up!

SDUDLA: They went with my husband. The pain of seeing these men in blue taking away my husband from us was like a blow in the eye. Where are you taking him to in the early hours of the morning?

POLICEMAN 1: None of your business.

SDUDLA: What did he do?

POLICEMAN 2: You dog. Don't pretend that you don't know.

SDUDLA: They took him away. What could I do – the bread-winner taken away; not knowing what was going to happen to him. The trial. The sentence: 15 years on the Island. In 1969 I was informed that my husband had died on the Island. Then my two sons went away. Where, I don't know. Some said they crossed the borders. I will never see them again. I don't know whether they are still alive. What could I do – my husband, my home, my sons – everything taken away from me. I was alone. But they can't destroy what is inside me. This world is full of plague. Plague! Hey, you, listen to me, it's fire, fire, fire everywhere.

She sings 'Lo Mzabalazo', *limps downstage and falls to the ground.*

Scene 9

THE HOSTEL

MAMBHELE: Look at this stupid Sdudla, she's mad, you know.

MAMPOMPO: I'm sick and tired of her.

MAMBHELE [*laughs*]: She's always carrying an umbrella. It is raining all the time for her.

MAMPOMPO: I'm not here to look after her. I am here to sell Mrs Ntlebi's chickens.

MAMBHELE: What does she think, must we sell her oranges and fat cakes? I'm not here for her. What she is always selling is politics.

MAMPOMPO: Politics. What is politics?

MAMBHELE: She was in Poqo, man.

MAMPOMPO: Politics makes me mad. Let's go and help her.

They pick SDUDLA *up and take her downstage right. Long pause.*

MAMBHELE: Mampompo, business is very bad today. I don't see any people. I'm worried [*silence*]. What about your husband, does he give any money?

MAMPOMPO: Oh yes, Nozulu is a very good man. He is earning R30 a week. R2 for bus fare, and he gives me R24, that is something.

MAMBHELE: That is something, mfazi, my husband is a nuisance in the house.

MAMPOMPO: Which one?

MAMBHELE: Hey, I don't like your jokes! My husband, Noma's father?

MAMPOMPO: Oh, I am sorry, I was just joking. Yes. I know Noma, she is the one who always comes here to fetch the heads and the chickens' legs. [*She laughs.*]

MAMBHELE: She is helping me a lot at home. My husband takes the money and drinks at the shebeen.

MAMPOMPO: Do you mean he is not working, taking the money? He is a nuisance, chuck him out of the house.

MAMBHELE: I wish I could, but you chuck this one out you get a worse one.

MAMPOMPO: Mambhele, I don't understand how men think. My husband can be funny if he wants to. When he came out of the hospital I was in Crossroads. He told me to go and stay with him in the hostel. [*She gestures for* MAMBHELE *to stand close and keeps on looking over her shoulder.*] Mambhele, you know there are a lot of men there. And the beds are like shelves and Nozulu's bed was on top. I had to take a stepladder. [*She gestures with her hand, indicating sexual intercourse.*]

MAMBHELE: But I thought he was too sick.

MAMPOMPO: Not for the Smarties [*gestures with hand*] my dear.

MAMBHELE: Where did he get the strength from?

MAMPOMPO: I didn't see him for two years.

MAMBHELE: For two years without Smarties, it's a long time.

MAMPOMPO: How can I do such a thing while people are eating and drinking, playing cards, moving around, not even a curtain to cover the bed?

MAMBHELE: What did you do then?

MAMPOMPO: I had no choice, he was demanding.

MAMBHELE: Oh I know, he accused you of having somebody in Transkei.

MAMPOMPO [*playing out the scene*]: But I didn't want to take off my clothes. He was very cross – he wanted me as I was born. Mambhele, I was just like a piece of wood, and the bed was making me nervous, eeee, eeee, it seemed louder than the wireless. Nozulu was jumping up and down, panting and grunting. Ooh Mambhele, I was pleased when it was over.

MAMBHELE: Ah, tog, you can't blame him for that after two years. He has been longing for you.

MAMPOMPO: I don't blame him, but that place is another thing. In the morning, after Nozulu got up to go to the clinic the man who was sleeping in the bed underneath asked me for Smarties. [*She gestures.*] I was shocked and told him, 'I'm a married woman'. He offered me money.

MAMBHELE: Did you say you are selling it?

MAMPOMPO: I told him to keep the money because I'm going to tell Nozulu when he is coming back. Later he told me he last saw his family in Transkei a long time back. I decided not to tell Nozulu about him.

MAMBHELE: I wouldn't like to sleep underneath while people are having Smarties on top. This hostel business is making us cheap. He wethu, were you also one of those women running from the hostels to the station early in the morning, running away from the inspectors?

MAMPOMPO: It was my daily bread, running to the station, sitting there for four hours. It was too much for me, then I told Nozulu to come and stay with me in Crossroads and I got that job I told you about on the farm.

SDUDLA [*looking into the distance*]: Hey . . . look at that smoke, there must be something happening.

MAMBHELE *and* MAMPOMPO: Hey, taxi man!

MAMBHELE: What is happening there?

MAMPOMPO: A blockade. What is happening?

MAMBHELE: There is no smoke without fire.

MAMPOMPO: Mambhele, there are no customers, even the taxis are empty.

MAMBHELE: Do you know how much I spent on these chickens? R50. I was supposed to make R40 profit. I owe Mhlozayo R20, I must buy wood and the supper for tonight.

MAMPOMPO: Hayi, hayi, I must stay here? I can be shot by a stray bullet while Mrs Ntlebi is sitting in her house.

SDUDLA: You can go home, it is trouble, here is also trouble, everywhere is trouble.

MAMPOMPO: Oh God, don't bring these troubles here.

MAMBHELE: I am worried about Noma selling the Zola Budds. My husband is troublesome, I can't get him out of my head, he turns my house upside down, and now this blockade.

Scene 10

THE FATHER

MAMPOMPO as FATHER. She wears a hat used to denote the character. SDUDLA as NOMA. NOMA runs into the house from outside to count her money. FATHER walks with a stick, has a limp, mimes smoking a cigarette. He comes into the room while NOMA is counting the money.

FATHER: Hello, Noma.

NOMA [*hiding the money*]: Hello, Tata.

FATHER: You know your father loves you very much, you look just like me. How was your business today?

NOMA: It went very well, Tata.

FATHER: How many chicken heads and legs did you sell today?

NOMA: About 30 legs and 20 heads.

FATHER: Mmmm, how much did you make?

NOMA: I don't know, I didn't count it yet.

FATHER: Your mother was just joking, give it to your Tata. I will count it.

NOMA: But Tata uyazi, if I give you this money Mama will give me a good hiding.

FATHER: Noma, give me the money, my friend is waiting for me. Give me the money so that I can go and buy something and we can cook before your mother comes home.

NOMA: Where are you going to, Tata?

FATHER: I am going to Madlamini's place with my friend.

NOMA [*withdrawing*]: You want me to give you Mama's money?

FATHER [*pulling the girl towards him*]: Look, Noma, I'm the boss in this bloody house. Your mother took my name. Remember the shoes I bought you.

NOMA [*cringing*]: Yes I do, Tata. But you are not working now.

FATHER: I'm going to get a job soon and then I will buy you a dress.

NOMA: When will that be, Tata?

FATHER: Soon, soon, my child, come to your father and give me the money.

> NOMA *shakes her head and tries to run away, mumbling under her breath.* FATHER *catches her.*

FATHER: Don't be silly. Give me the money and I will give you some back.

NOMA [*shaking her head and mumbling under her breath*]: But Tata, my mother will give me a big punishment. I can't.

FATHER: You are only 12 years old and you want to give me orders in my house. Give me the money. Give me the money!

> *They struggle and he takes the money.* NOMA *cries.*

FATHER: Don't worry, I'll bring some back.

> *He exits and* NOMA *sobs, going down on her hands and knees.*

NOMA: I don't know what I am going to say to my mother.

MAMBHELE [*offstage*]: Noma. [*She is tired after a day's work.*] Noma!

NOMA [*wiping her eyes and pretending not to be crying*]: Hello, Mama.

MMBHELE: What happened to your eyes?

NOMA [*trying to hide her face*]: I've got a terrible headache, Mama.

MAMBHELE: But you look as if you have been crying. Have you been crying? [*No reply*] I can see you have been crying. Ag, I'm so tired, please bring me a bankie to sit on. I've been working in the hot sun the whole day. Make me some tea, please.

NOMA *brings a drum and* MAMBHELE *sits downstage left.*

NOMA [*under her breath*]: There is no paraffin, Mama, for the stove, Mama.

MAMBHELE: Give me the money so that you can go and buy paraffin. [NOMA *starts to cry.*] Give me the money. Noma, give me the money!

NOMA: Tata took all the money.

MAMBHELE: Don't talk nonsense. I told you not to give your father . . .

NOMA: He forced me to give it to him, Mama.

MAMBHELE: You don't listen to me. Where has your father gone to?

NOMA: To Madlamini's place, Mama.

MAMBHELE: Oh! He is going to spend all my money on the drink. All day I'm working hard selling chickens, smiling even if I don't want to smile, laughing even if I don't want to. Men are touching me and I am still laughing. I'm working for you and your brothers. I come home tired and I must cook, your father is demanding a plate of food from me. Work all day and work all night.

I must look after the house, clean, wash, iron, while your father is drinking my money at Madlamini's place. I can't tolerate this anymore. Uyandinyela. He is shitting on my head.

NOMA [*still crying*]: Please don't be cross with me.

MAMBHELE: Thula, thula, let me think. I want to think. Thula! Alright my baby, it's alright. Stop crying. Whew, what can I do – shh – shh. [*She sings a song and plays with* NOMA'*s hair.*]

UMadlamini undimoshile
Ngokuthath'imali yabantwana bam.
Ndiyamzonda, Ndiyamzonda
Ngokuthath' imali yabantwana bam.

MAMBHELE: You know, your father was not always like this. He was a driver, my child.

NOMA: I remember, Mama, once he even came with the van and took us for a drive.

MAMBHELE: You remember, your father was a good husband and sometimes helped me in the house. Those days seem so long ago. Then he had his accident.

NOMA: Mama, I remember Tata lying in the big, smelling hospital with his broken leg. I was so frightened of those nurses in white, Ma.

MAMBHELE: Why didn't he have his accident on his way to work? Why did he have to break his leg on his way home after work?

NOMA: Why, Mama?

MAMBHELE: If he had had his accident on his way to work we would have got worker's compensation.

NOMA: What is that, Ma?

MAMBHELE: Money, my child.

NOMA: And now?

MAMBHELE: Nothing, nothing, my child. That accident was like a punishment in our family. It seems as if someone is wishing bad luck on us.

NOMA: But Tata could have gone back to his job when he came out of hospital.

MAMBHELE: He did go there, my child, he was told there were no vacancies. At first your father was seriously looking for a job. I started this business of chicken selling. Later he would take the bus fare I gave him and buy beer. That is when he started his business of drinking, so I decided not to give him anymore money.

MAMPOMPO, *making the sound of a helicopter, enters on the back rostrum.*

NOMA [*looking at the helicopter and pointing*]: Ma, Mama, nansti: laa ntaka.

She runs away.

MAMBHELE [*to the helicopter*]: I've got enough troubles in my life without you. You are a monster that separates us. Our children are afraid of you and you have caused them to live in fear. You have taken their childhood away from them and made them into mongrels.

NOMA: It is always spying on us, Mama.

MAMPOMPO: I hate you. People fight against each other because of you. You are a vulture that sweeps down on our innocent people. Since you are here there is no peace.

During this speech NOMA *transforms back into* SDUDLA.

Scene 11

THE FOREBODING BIRD

MAMBHELE: I wish that thing would go away. I'm losing money. My chickens will be bad. Since this mzabalazo has begun my business has gone from bad to worse. Trouble here, trouble at home.

Enter SDUDLA.

SDUDLA: You think the struggle started now? It started a long time ago. It started with our forefathers, Hintsa, Ngqika, Mshweshwe and Dingane.

MAMPOMPO: Sdudla, what are you talking about? Are you telling me about men who are dead a long time ago? Is Dingane going to help me now to get to Crossroads?

SDUDLA: If you don't want to listen now it does not matter, but the day will come when you will listen.

MAMPOMPO: Mambhele, it's better for you because your house is not so far from here. How am I going to get to Crossroads? There is no transport. Nozulu won't listen to this story. I haven't even cooked for him.

MAMBHELE: My house is near, but when the trouble starts it is difficult to get there. I'm standing here thinking of my two sons. Did they come home safe from school?

SDUDLA: When there is a blockade here, Langa, Nyanga, Gugulethu, it is everywhere. No one can get in, and no one can get out.

MAMPOMPO: I'm waiting for Mrs Ntlebi to come and give me my money. She must give me R2. She will say something because I sold few chickens. There is no bonus today for me. The money that Nozulu and I earn is not enough for us to live on, never mind sending to my children in Transkei. I last sent money home three months ago and it wasn't enough. I wonder how they are managing.

MAMBHELE: I don't know who to contact first if I want money – the whole township is full of my debts; people are getting tired of lending me money. I was hoping to make a big profit so that I can buy my younger son a pair of shoes and pay back some of the people I owe money to. [*She jokes.*] Hayi mfazi, I've been thinking my children will be social workers, lawyers, doctors. He wethu, I can't even afford to buy a pair of shoes, ha!

MAMPOMPO: He mfazi zala uzoxoxa. I thought that my children would be teachers and nurses, but I don't have money to feed them.

SDUDLA: You spend your time worrying about money and chickens – money and chickens. That is all that is on your mind.

MAMBHELE: You always talk to us about politics. I can't worry with politics. I must look after my children and I want to live quietly.

SDUDLA: Don't talk nonsense, politics comes into everything. What you want is peace, but what you get is another thing.

MAMBHELE: If you are a mother what can you do? You live in fear that your children won't grow up well. Fear that your children might come to harm. We live in fear from day to day. I must worry about my chickens and money because chickens mean money to me and money is my children's future.

MAMPOMPO: I left my children in Transkei. They are starving. I came to Cape Town to look for work so that I could get some money to feed them. [*She turns to* SDUDLA.] You have no feeling of a mother, you are staying alone in the backyard of other people's houses, no children, nothing to worry about.

SDUDLA: Do you know who you are?

MAMPOMPO: Yes, I know myself. I'm Nozulu's wife – umfazi kaNozulu.

SDUDLA: Is that all you know about yourself?

MAMPOMPO: I also know how to make money, like selling the chickens. When I've got money I'll go back to Transkei, build myself a big house, educate my children, buy myself a farm with a tractor and be my own boss.

SDUDLA: Mampompo, you've got a dream that will never come true.

MAMPOMPO: My dream will come true because Baba Botha has taken the pass away.

SDUDLA: Have you forgotten that you can't read or write? Do you think you can get a better job? Mampompo, you are going to work and work and work until you die. The system hasn't changed, the root is deep in the soil. We are still struggling, fighting against oppression, we are forced to obey laws in which we have no part or say in the making.

MAMPOMPO: The laws are made here in Cape Town.

SDUDLA: The laws which forced you to leave your children behind and come here to be a chicken slaughterer. The laws which keep our sons and daughters behind bars. How many have died under this law? For it is made by a human being for another human being. What has it caused us – pain, sorrow, destruction? We carry a heavy burden that defeats men but won't defeat women.

She sings 'Umthwalo'.

Unzima lo mthwalo
Woyis' amadoda
Angeke soyiswe
Ke thina bafazi

Scene 12

THE BLOCKADE

The cast makes the sounds of Casspirs, Hippos and the singing of 'Die Stem'.

MAMPOMPO: Nazi! Nazi! A Hippo! They are coming to our township like a line of ants. [*She sings* 'Die Stem'.]

SDUDLA: What law is this? What race of men? What is this? You make weapons to give you the strength that you lack; you enslave us, whip us, use chains or guns at your pleasure. Do you think we are cows to go on bearing children for you to yoke or kill? What you are unable to create you destroy.

MAMBHELE: Hey! White boy, what are you thinking of, as you sit there like a king on top of the Casspir? Have you forgotten your black mother, who cleaned up your vomit when you were sick?

MAMPOMPO: Or dried your tears when you were crying? We kissed the sores and scratches on your small body to make them better, because your white mother was too busy playing tennis, or shopping.

MAMBHELE: How many of your shit nappies have I changed? You have shown us what you want in our township . . . killing only!

MAMPOMPO: Our children grow up with hate and fear.

MAMBHELE: They have spoilt our children. They have shown them things that children shouldn't know about. To kill without respect for a human life.

MAMPOMPO: They have torn our families apart – everything is upside down.

MAMBHELE: It is the children who are telling the parents what to do.

MAMPOMPO: Didn't I tell you about these children? Running around the township, no mothers to look after them. Growing up with no laws.

SDUDLA: These, my children, who spill blood as easy as saying voetsek; created by the system and the men in blue who protect it. These are not the children who we laboured to give birth to and held in our arms but the monsters created by the system of oppression.

MAMPOMPO: Thula, thula. I hear voices.

MAMBHELE: There is someone speaking from the bird in the sky.

MAMPOMPO: I can't hear what he is saying – thula! Thula!

SDUDLA [*going to sit on a drum*]: Ag man, once they speak from the bird I know that they are only giving us orders. Don't listen to them.

MAMPOMPO: Hey, Sdudla, man, I want to hear! Shhhh . . . Listen! It's that white man. He is speaking in Xhosa. Is he speaking about the funeral again?

MAMBHELE: Yes, the funeral. Only the family can go.

MAMPOMPO: No! No! Mambhele, the funeral is not only for the family but for everybody.

MAMBHELE: Shut up, man! No organisation flags, no salutes, no placards – nobody must carry the coffin on their shoulders, it must go in the hearse.

MAMPOMPO: Why don't they let us bury our dead in peace?

MAMBHELE: Do you see they are opening a door underneath?

MAMPOMPO: Aah . . . a white bomb!

They run around the stage. MAMPOMPO *hides behind* MAMBHELE.

MAMBHELE: Hayi, hayi, Mampompo – papers, pamphlets. Come, Sdudla.

SDUDLA [*uninterested and sitting on her drum*]: Ah! Voetsek, you are running around like your chickens without heads.

MAMBHELE [*reading a pamphlet with difficulty*]: 'A policeman is a friend, he is there to protect you, and see that order is maintained.'

MAMPOMPO: A friend? He used to chase us out of the hostel early in the morning. Was he a friend then?

MAMBHELE: Does a friend let you sleep in jail for selling chickens? When did he start to be a friend? When he took my money and my chickens, put me in the van like a bird in a cage and drove around with me all day?

SDUDLA: Is the juice of the orange starting to work now?

MAMPOMPO: I'm tired of these men in blue pushing us around, telling us what to do.

MAMBHELE [*tears up the pamphlet*]: Iyuu Mampompo, I hear children singing freedom songs. Look, look, everybody is running away. [*She starts singing.*]

Hayi Hayi
Nantsi imello yello
Imello yello [*repeat three times*]
Izosidubula
Dubula [*repeat twice*]
Balekani [*repeat twice*]

Scene 13

THE STUDENT PROTEST

As students, the cast sing a protest song and toyi-toyi on the spot, miming carrying guns.

> Lenj' uBotha isiqhel' amasimba ngokubulalisa
> Isizwe sethu
> Sizozibulala ezi zinja

The three actors change back into their main characters.

MAMBHELE [*speaking over the song*]: Why must they come this way? Why didn't they take the other way?

MAMPOMPO: I told you a long time ago that these children are troublemakers; these songs mean trouble.

SDUDLA: It is not the songs that cause the trouble but the Casspirs.

MAMPOMPO: I can't go to my place in Crossroads and I can't leave these chickens here. I'm afraid of dying.

MAMBHELE: What do these children want? Maybe they are going to the dead comrade's place to say a prayer.

MAMPOMPO: They were asked not to be there; they are just looking for trouble.

SDUDLA: Mampompo, you must choose which side you are on. Our children are not frightened, they criss-cross the streets from yard to yard. They are not frightened by these police. If they run they are shot; if they walk they are arrested.

MAMBHELE: Let me try and do something before these children come here. I can't lose my chickens . . .

MAMPOMPO: Hey, Mambhele! The children have stopped singing.

MAMBHELE: It is right on top of us.

MAMPOMPO: The plague bird is making a big wind around us and everything is moving around.

They huddle together.

SDUDLA: It has been circling over us all day waiting to snatch its prey. We see you and we are not frightened.

MAMBHELE: It won't go away until the Casspir has gone.

MAMPOMPO: Nkosi yam, it's moving away. Now maybe the children are going to another place. I'm running away now.

SDUDLA: Mampompo, if you don't stay you will find yourself carrying stones as if you never bore children.

MAMPOMPO: My children are not here, they are all in Transkei.

MAMBHELE: You are selfish.

SDUDLA: These are all our children. Can't you see we are living the lives of chickens waiting to be killed?

MAMPOMPO [*turning upstage*]: The Casspirs are around us. I can't go anywhere.

MAMBHELE: They are blocking off the road. They won't let the students go through.

MAMPOMPO: The children are starting to sing again.

MAMBHELE: The soldiers are giving them five minutes to disperse. Why don't they run and go back? [*She turns to the children, arms outstretched, begging them.*] Please go . . . go! Hambani! Hambani! Hambani! They won't listen, Mampompo. Look, that child is running away.

MAMPOMPO: The soldier is running after her. Please don't shoot!!! [*She raises her hands.*]

MAMBHELE: She is only a child. Her hands are empty. She is only a child. Her hands are empty.

MAMPOMPO: Don't shoot! Please don't!

MAMBHELE: Please!

SDUDLA: Don't shoot . . . Don't . . .

MAMBHELE: Don't shoot, please don't shoot . . . [*The child is shot. Silence.*] I have been seeing this thing for a long time. Bloodshed all around me and I have done nothing. Today is somebody else's child, tomorrow mine.

MAMPOMPO: I'm standing here without my children. Alone, watching these young soldiers killing children like flies. How long are you going to do this to us? How long are we going to allow you to do this to us?

SDUDLA: For more than 100 years our people came to you in peace, but you refused to listen; 30 years ago thousands of women marched to Pretoria in peace, but you refused to see us or listen to us. Our leaders came in peace and you arrested them. At Sharpeville we came in peace, you shot us. Baphi?

MAMBHELE *and* MAMPOMPO: Shiya hom, hom bhasophani. Shiya hom, hom bhasophani.

MAMPOMPO: Baphi – we will go and, by God, we will win.

SDUDLA: We will storm the Bastille of Pollsmoor. Baphi?

MAMPOMPO: Caledon Square!

ALL: Baphi?

SDUDLA: John Vorster Square!

MAMBHELE: Nongqongqo!

SDUDLA: Modderbee!

ALL: Baphi? Pollsmoor!!!

SDUDLA *and* MAMBHELE: The sun will rise for all the working women in the world.

They all pick up sticks and use them as if they were doing traditional stick fighting.

ALL TOGETHER [*singing*]: He Botha, He Botha man

Uzama ukwenzani xa uthint' abafazi
Wathint' abafazi, wathint' imbokotho!

Discussion Points

- What does the play teach us about the 1956 Women's March and from what viewpoint? What are the slogans written on placards or included in the anthem sung by the women? How do these compare with slogans – written, spoken and sung – used in protests today?
- What information is recorded in your identity document and/or passport? What do these documents represent and how do they differ from the dompas? What does the play teach us about the dompas and the system of social segregation it supported?
- What does the play say about the way the roles women perform define them in terms of their relationships with men? In what ways do the women resist these roles and expectations?
- In what ways does the text incorporate the distinction between local urban/township experiences and those in rural areas? Why is this important? What details of each character's individual history distinguish her personality and behaviour?
- The stage directions indicate a 'non-realistic' neutral space in which the props are mimed. What are the advantages of this style of presentation?
- Bertolt Brecht championed using historical incidents and settings in order to write plays that challenged the political processes of his own time. He favoured detachment or 'distance' that would enable an audience to think critically about issues rather than simply become caught up

in the emotions evoked by the play. He used various techniques to achieve this sense of distancing. Three Brechtian strategies are used in this play: the montage of scenes, each of which is more or less autonomous; the introduction of song to interrupt the flow of action; and the use of scene titles. The Brechtian-style scene titles indicate that the sketches focus on episodes or situations beyond the immediate present. How do the scene titles locate or anchor scenes and character experiences in this play?

- Ordinary life is set against a backdrop of constant military and police presence. What are some of the indicators of state presence?
- The play integrates vernacular with English. What is the effect of this linguistic intertwining? The action is also punctuated with songs. What is the effect of this pattern?

www.ingramcontent.com/pod-product-compliance
Lightning Source LLC
LaVergne TN
LVHW051013080826
845145LV00009B/2595

* 9 7 8 1 7 7 6 1 4 7 2 0 5 *